Dzine
PUNK FUNK

Dzine: *Punk Funk*

Published by
Contemporary Art Museum St. Louis
3750 Washington Boulevard
St. Louis, Missouri 63108

This publication was prepared on the occasion of the exhibition
Dzine: *Punk Funk*
March 18 – July 17, 2005
Organized by Shannon Fitzgerald, Chief Curator, for the Contemporary Art Museum St. Louis.

Contemporary Art Museum St. Louis acknowledges the generous funding support for the exhibition and catalog awarded by the Whitaker Foundation, Monique Meloche Gallery, Chicago, SCAI the Bathhouse/Shiraishi Contemporary Art Inc., Tokyo, Regional Arts Commission, Arts & Education Council, and Friends of the Museum, with in-kind support from the Chase Park Plaza Hotel.

ISBN 0-9712195-7-5
Library of Congress Control Number: 2005923743

Edited by Ivy Cooper
Design by Bruce Burton, Graphic Designer, Contemporary Art Museum St. Louis

Printed by Nies/Artcraft, St. Louis
Printed and bound in St. Louis

Available through
D.A.P. / Distributed Art Publishers
155 Sixth Avenue, 2nd Floor,
New York, N.Y. 10013
Tel: (212) 627-1999 Fax: (212) 627-9484

Cover: *Punk Funk*, 2005, acrylic, Envirotex, and varnish on wood mount attached to wall, 14 x 42 feet. Courtesy of the artist, Monique Meloche Gallery, Chicago, SCAI the Bathhouse/ Shiraishi Contemporary Art Inc., Tokyo, and realized with the assistance of Contemporary Art Museum St. Louis.

Dzine

PUNK FUNK

March 18 — July 17, 2005

TABLE OF CONTENTS

Director's Acknowledgments

This catalog accompanies *Punk Funk*, a solo exhibition by Chicago based artist Dzine at the Contemporary Art Museum St. Louis. Dzine created new works for the exhibition, including a 14 x 42 foot site specific piece, his largest and most ambitious work to date. We are very fortunate that Dzine chose to feature this new work in this exhibition at the Contemporary making for such a remarkable project. I am grateful for his leap of faith and for accepting the Contemporary as his partner. The exhibition reaffirms the Contemporary's continued commitment to groundbreaking exhibitions and to commissioning new work. I am grateful to Dzine for providing us with his installation and am proud to bring his work to the public. I am also indebted to the Contemporary's Chief Curator Shannon Fitzgerald for her tireless efforts to discover and champion new talent.

Our sincere thanks to the individuals who agreed to lend the works, as well as the funders whose generosity made the exhibition and the accompanying catalog possible. The Contemporary extends our thanks and appreciation to the lenders of the exhibition;

Sigrid and Jeffery Brooks, St. Louis; Donald L. Bryant, Jr. Family Art Trust, St. Louis; Andrew and Mary Ann Srenco, St. Louis; and Sara Szold, Chicago. I want to thank Monique Meloche and the Monique Meloche Gallery, Chicago, and Maho Kubota and Mr. Shiraishi and the SCAI the Bathhouse/Shiraishi Contemporary Art Inc., Tokyo, for helping to fund the exhibition and catalog. For their continued support, I am grateful to Christy Gray and the Whitaker Foundation, Jill McGuire and the Regional Arts Commission, Jim Weidman and Arts & Education Council, and finally the all the Friends of the Museum. Additional thanks to Maya Romanoff, Chicago, DJ Cam and Inflammable Records, Paris.

As always, the entire Contemporary's staff contributed immeasurably to make Dzine's exhibition a success. I want to thank the local artists for their vital contributions in helping Dzine with the work.

In closing, I thank Dzine for taking risks with his art making and giving us the opportunity to present it.

Paul Ha
Director

Curator's Acknowledgments

Dzine: *Punk Funk* is possible because of the support and enthusiasm of the board and staff at the Contemporary. I extend my sincere gratitude to Paul Ha, Director, who has been supportive and receptive to this project from its inception. Brandon Anschultz and Michael Schuh have been instrumental to the installation and organizational details of the exhibition—I am grateful for their skills, their willingness, and sense of humor. I appreciate the assistance of Andrea Green, Mark McLeod, and Allyson Ross for the many tasks they do on a daily basis that help makes things happen. Thanks to Kelly Scheffer and Susan Lee for their creative education initiatives and outreach in the community. Many thanks to our amazing group of adult docents from the Contemporary Art Partnership who make tours exciting! Additional thanks are due to Susan Werremeyer, Lisa Grove, Mary Walters, Jason Miller, Boo McLoughlin, Jennifer Daly, and Cole Root who have contributed in numerous ways.

Special thanks to Bruce Burton, Graphic Designer, for his ability to bring the art and music of this exhibition together in such an innovative and stunning catalog. I extend a warm thanks to editor Ivy Cooper, whose wordsmith and patience was of great help and to Brigitte Foley for her valuable feedback and additional set of eyes. Additional thanks and appreciation go to Maya Romanoff for his spectacular collaboration with Dzine on several works in the exhibition; Jesse De La Peña for his work on the CD; Jay Fram and Blyth Renate Meier for use of their wonderful photographs of Dzine's work; and to Peter Doroshenko for his support and advocacy of Dzine.

The creation of the site-specific work *Punk Funk* occurred over a two week period. I want to thank the talented team of artists who worked with us on the exhibition. In St. Louis: Brandon Anschultz, Sharon Cox, Sandra Marchewa, Paul Shank, Erik Spehn, Kiersten Torres, and Sarah Ursini, and in Chicago: Marissa Baker, Louis Barak, Dominique Maciejka, and Jeff Zimmerman. It was enormously rewarding to witness daily the collaborative spirit that brought *Punk Funk* to fruition—Thank You!

For their generosity, support, and thoughts, I am grateful to Monique Meloche of Monique Meloche Gallery, Chicago, and Maho Kubota at SCAI the Bathhouse/Shiraishi Contemporary Art Inc., Tokyo. Their efforts in the realization of this project were considerable.

I want to extend my thanks to DJ Cam for creating the magical and ambient CD, *The Lost Kingdom* that accompanies the exhibition and this catalog. I greatly appreciate the generosity of Cam and Inflamable Records for sharing such fluid and remarkable compositions that truly enrich the experiential nature of Dzine's work.

Finally, I would like to convey my heartfelt thanks to Dzine, for creating such a dynamic body of work for the Contemporary. Dzine's paintings are spontaneous, sexy, energetic, and engulfing in the best way. I thank Dzine for his energy toward this project, as it was thrilling to work together and literally watch and listen as *Punk Funk* unfolded.

Shannon Fitzgerald
Chief Curator

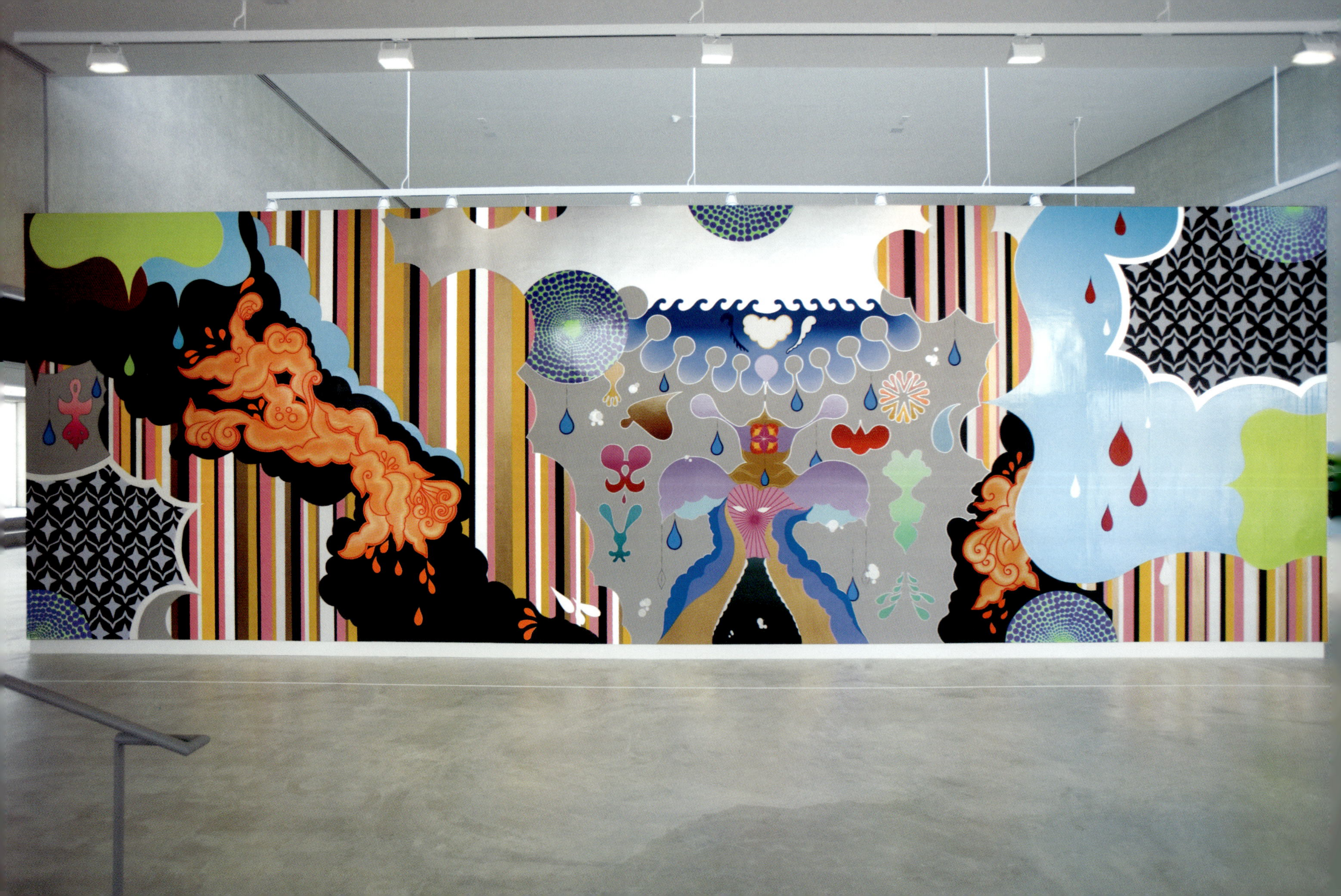

Dzine's *Punk Funk: A Wayward Fusion*

Shannon Fitzgerald

Chicago-based artist Dzine is a painter and the owner of an experimental record label that has worked with world renowned DJs and producers such as DJ Cam, Gotan Project, Yellow Productions, and Guidance Recordings. Straddling the very thin boundary between art and music, Dzine creates abstract, biological, morphing forms that vibrate with intense color. This exhibition, *Punk Funk*, includes a 14 x 42 foot site-specific, mural-like painting, a series of new acrylic paintings, and a new music soundtrack. These elements create an environment that makes energy visible and unleashes a unique rhythm and lyricism.

As a young artist, Dzine was inspired by the New York graffiti movement and began painting on the streets of Chicago at the age of thirteen. He later became an important component of Chicago's early hip hop scene in the late 1980s and early 90s.[1] Dzine's first "canvas" was public space, outdoor walls that led to an understanding of surfaces and technique that now inform his distinctive approach to handling materials, imagery, and scale and perspective. Fred Brathwaite offered insight to this critical period in Dzine's artistic development:

Many of today's leading art and design talents began their artistry with trains and spray cans. In the 70s and 80s, the urban subway and elevated train lines worked double duty for these artists, serving as both canvas and mobile art exhibition. After the 80s, however, many of these artists grew beyond using spray paint and train cars to create their work.[2]

Inspired by the artists Brathwaite refers to (Rammellzee, Futura, and Lee Quionnes, among others), Dzine was also interested in Abstract Expressionists (Twombly, Schnabel, Richter, and later Basquiat), and he began to fuse the animation of his paintings with a wide range of musical references to develop his own visual language that combined line, color, beats per minutes (BPM), and world culture in an innovative way. Since the late 1990s, Dzine has been displacing historical styles and recycling them into a rapidly evolving yet recognizable expressive voice.

His most recent work moves between a purposeful roughness and a refined and sophisticated formalism. These binaries are balanced in both expansive and tightly compressed spaces and introduced in parts that act like moving fractals or sound samples. Interested in sensory fusion, particularly between sound and vision, Dzine creates visually stunning and evocative paintings that are sometimes accompanied by a soundtrack. At the Contemporary, the ambient sounds that fill the gallery space are composed by Paris-based DJ Cam. DJ Cam and Dzine responded to one another's work to create an emotional and atmospheric experience.

Dzine applies a layer of Envirotex (a thick, clear plastic coating) onto the surface to complete his slick, abstract paintings. Recently, he's also incorporated tiny glass beads (made in collaboration with designer Maya Romanoff) to give the work a layered, jewel-like effect. The addition of these reflective (and decorative) materials to otherwise super-flat forms (dots, stripes, drips, etc.) creates an alluring depth and evoke bling, glitz, glimmer, and glamour.

In other work, his pulsating surfaces also treat compulsive repetition (base lines, drum beats) as pointillist obsessions, gothic doodling, and radiating spheres existing in between the slick layers of Envirotex. As a collector of materials and textures, Dzine joins the unnatural (the toxic, plastic material) and the natural (the manual labor of sanding and smoothing) in a kind of dialectical layering of creative forces. The layers act both as see-through veils and protective surfaces that, through their dazzling and reflective quality, allow entry for the viewer. Notions of conceal and reveal are constantly at play in Dzine's work. Yet despite the optical allusions (and illusions), mesmerizing and distracting patterns, and layers of reflective surfaces, the ultimate goal of the work is the achievement of transparency and lucid revelations.

Dzine says of this new direction in his work:

> The new body of work stems from my exploration of the term optic -- the effect of color and light. I am interested in how some paintings make the eye vibrate and in some cases the viewer needs to physically move left to right to view the intricacies in the painting that appear and disappear depending on the treatment of the surfaces with either the slick, glossy Envirotex or the delicate glass beads.
>
> This is a natural progression from my ambition of "synesthesia." There is an optical illusion allowed by a heavy pour of Envirotex over the surface of my paintings that creates a false three-dimensionality in the work. The painting *To be Continued* is a good example and the first time I have actually applied paint in between multiple layers of Envirotex. When viewed from a distance, this painting looks like a solid monochrome minimalist work. However, thousands of pink dots are laboriously painted in between the Envirotex layers taking it into a different direction that makes it vibrate/reverberate/pulsate. The painting continues to morph and the light starts to play a big factor giving it a wet floating sensation -- also giving the painting the effect of multiple layers of color, when in fact, only one pink is used. So in essence you have the real layers on top of the "suggested" depth further confounded by actual shadows of the dots within the layers. The optic illusion culminates with the highly reflective surface.[3]

The title piece, *Punk Funk*, is the artist's largest work to date. The artist's multi-layered approach to painting plays with traditional notions of perspective. His surfaces possess a push/pull tension combined with mesmerizing optics that work to express visual sound bubbles and music as lingering sensation. Dzine's visual language presents a dialogue that is harmonious and corporal, as opposed to the hard-edge, hard-core expressions he sometimes references. The title *Punk Funk* refers to ways in which his work investigates the languages of two expressive subculture movements—Punk and Funk—and fuses aspects of each: syncopated rhythms, repetitive bass lines, notions of social alienation, and youth rebellion. While Funk is largely understood today as a middle-aged black male movement, and Punk became a largely a white suburban youth movement, Dzine works to capture the staying power and energies of both styles. Interested in the visceral experience of Punk and Funk (and Punk Funk) the artist incorporates the energy of each to create a visual mélange that suggests a sensual, even hallucinogenic, evolution of experience. This is reinforced by the titles the artist assigns his work (purposefully misspelled), with some taken from Cam's tracks: *Love Junkee*, *Friends & Enemies*, *To be Continued* and

opposite page:
Punk Funk, 2005, installation view at the Contemporary Art Museum St. Louis. Photo: Bruce Burton.

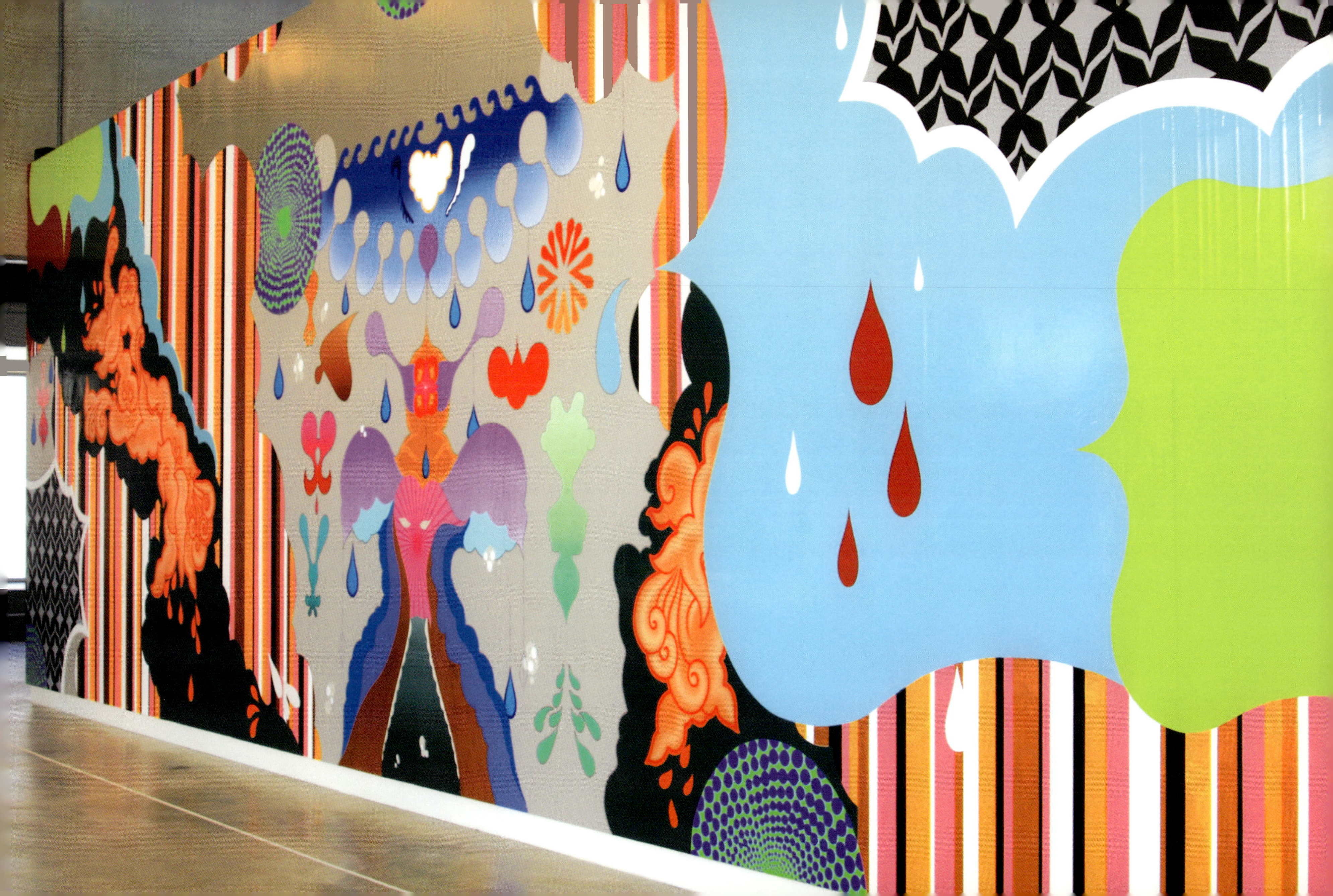

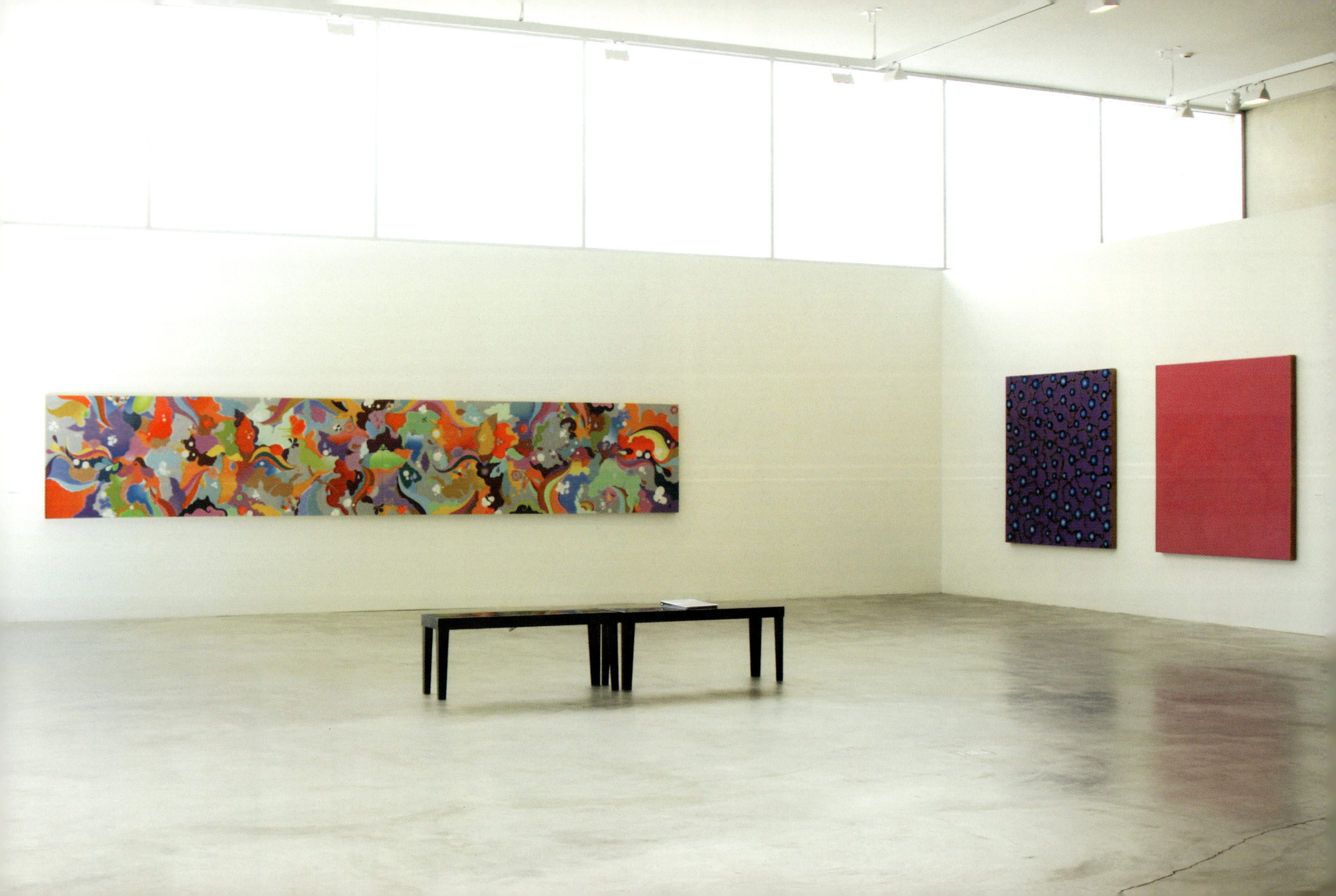

Untitled Interludes from the Optik Series. On an earlier project combining music and painting titled *Sampler* at the Museum of Contemporary Art, Chicago, curator Jerome Sans wrote of Dzine's ability to fuse image and sound:

> Be able to listen-see or see-listen. The connection between eyes and ears is physical. Senses work in combination, connect, and create a more complete perception. There is a common esthetic experience in between what you see and what you hear. It is all about a vibration to an external signal which is increased when senses proceed simultaneously . . . Visual artists turn the notion of illustration into something that says "what you see is about what you will hear" and contribute to visually interpret a certain music style, create a group graphic identity, and define an esthetic for music.[4]

Having collaborated together before, Dzine and DJ Cam remain interested in the emotive qualities of visual and sound movements and how each informs the other. In a continuation of this exploration and exchange of ideas, DJ Cam's track, *The Lost Kingdom*, emphasizes the transformative attributes of music and painting; the melding of the two produces a visualization of color and sound, a new synesthesia. Created specifically for this exhibition, *The Lost Kingdom* includes the tracks *friends and enemies*, *twilight zone*, *angel dust* and *hip hop pioneers*, and interjected with breaks called *essence part one*, *essence part two*-through four that act as interludes. Added to this compilation are samples featuring international fusion and remixes by Thievery Corporation, Kenny Dope, Cameo, J Dilla, Kakoli Sengupta, and Filet of Soul that emphasize a universality of influence and form that Dzine instills in his paintings. Known for innovatively layering his music with "sprinkles of dub, jazz, and soundtrack-y type ambience," DJ Cam's "minimalist approach, coupled with downbeat instrumental trip-hop built from obscure samples and stomp-box turntable accompaniments re-birth themselves into artfully arranged compositions" provides a smooth finish to Dzine's installation.[5]

Dzine chose to collaborate with DJ Cam because his creative work with groups and producers like Massive Attack, DJ Krush, and DJ Shadow, acknowledged Punk Funk along the way. Dzine expresses that "his wonderful, spontaneous, abstract, and slick production that involves lush layers of trumpets, piano, samples, psychedelia, and some trip-hop, echo and evoke strategies I enjoy and employ in my own work, which is likewise layered and very slick."

The painting *Love Junkee* represents Dzine's interest in translating the flow and layering of rhythm with very flat colors. The title is taken from DJ Cam's track featuring Cameo (another funk pioneer) included on the accompanying limited edition CD. According to Dzine, "the final addition of applying the tiny glass beads (in three sizes) then creates a different sensation of layering and depth not allowed with paint, it lends the work a sculptural presence of jewels, love and bling! 'punk funk'. . ."

Dzine's layers of undulating forms halted by rigid tides and bold colors correspond to the layers of DJ Cam's music; each layer of paint and pour of Envirotext relates to BPM. Dzine states, "My work has always had this sort of musical balance and I've always painted to music, but I needed something that would allow me to layer paint the way a music producer layers a track."[6]

opposite page:
Punk Funk, 2005, installation view at the Contemporary Art Museum St. Louis. Photo: Bruce Burton.

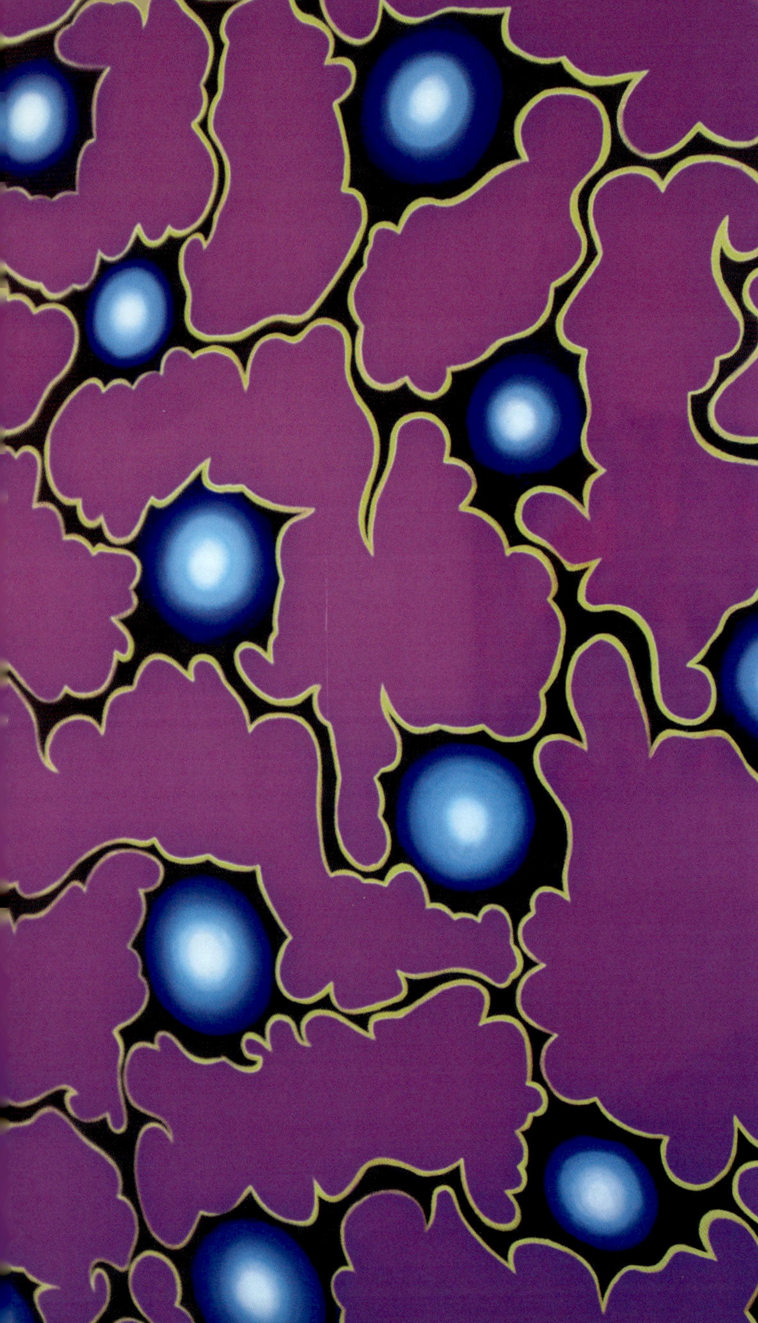

As DJ Cam arranges compositions comprised of often disparate elements, Dzine likewise builds from unexpected combinations. His compositions are in many ways a wayward fusion about opposites—delivered with a unique staccato harmony. His arrangements assert that spontaneity can be systematically devised, mathematical rules may be random, cultural appropriation is constantly creating new hybrids, and spirituality may be resistant to guidance or discipline. Interested in life's wonderful contrary moments, Dzine makes paintings that are both beautiful and simple at once. They are surface rich while communicating an underlying depth. While his work is prompted by caprice and appears to stray from rules of painting (and theory), it is an orchestration of purposeful impulses.

Dzine is a builder, constructing visual language through physical and conceptual layers, employing arrangements of color, form, abstraction and sound. He uses materials like acrylic, metallic, silver and copper paint, and layers of resin to render paintings like collages, communicating meaningful phrases, clauses, and sentences. His compositions (wayward fusions) are marked by deviations that move full circle from the willful to the unexpected, but remain desirable and gratifying. Dzine shares affinities with many of his contemporaries in this manner. He is part of a generation of painters that includes Ingrid Calame and Katharina Grosse, whose mural paintings and site-specific work similarly explore color, emotion, and location in abstract language; the spontaneity of Barry McGee and the late Margaret Killgallen; and Ryan McGinness, who likewise employs a DIY aesthetic and embraces his "outsider" (skateboard & surf culture) aesthetic.

Equally interested in design and the history of pattern, motif, and color, Dzine incorporates these references in a seemingly random manner. In his paintings one finds everything from lotus flowers, pinwheels, teardrops, floating radials (shields, discs, halo, the sun) covered in dots, to designers' logos (such as the Louis Vuitton monogram). His infusion of design quotes architecture, interiors, and fashion in revealing layers. Included in the new work is a 1960s psychedelic pop sensibility (particularly the swirling color forms and concentric circling of Scandanavian design known as *Abstracta*), Striped wall paper accompanied by large target motifs in various shades of 1960s and 70s Pantone colors (reminiscent of shag pile rugs), and even space-age atomic pop art and other futuristic renderings. His paintings are in part "a color clash of psychedelic music, sex and fashion. I wanted to create an installation which considered these elements in a fusion of painting and music that pulsate with a rhythm and a bit of irony that reflects culture that developed during that time period and remains influential."

Dzine strikes a balance between the vernacular and spiritual references in a celebratory fashion. This exhibition is a continuation of a hypnotic confluence as recently noted by Peter Doroshenko:

Friends and Enemies (detail), Photo: Bruce Burton.

opposite page:
Friends and Enemies and *To be Continued*, 2005, acrylic and Envirotex on canvas on wood mount, 70 x 70 inches. Courtesy of the artist, Monique Meloche Gallery, Chicago, and SCAI the Bathhouse/Shiraishi Contemporary Art Inc. Photo: Bruce Burton.

To be Continued (detail). Photo: Blyth Renate Meier.

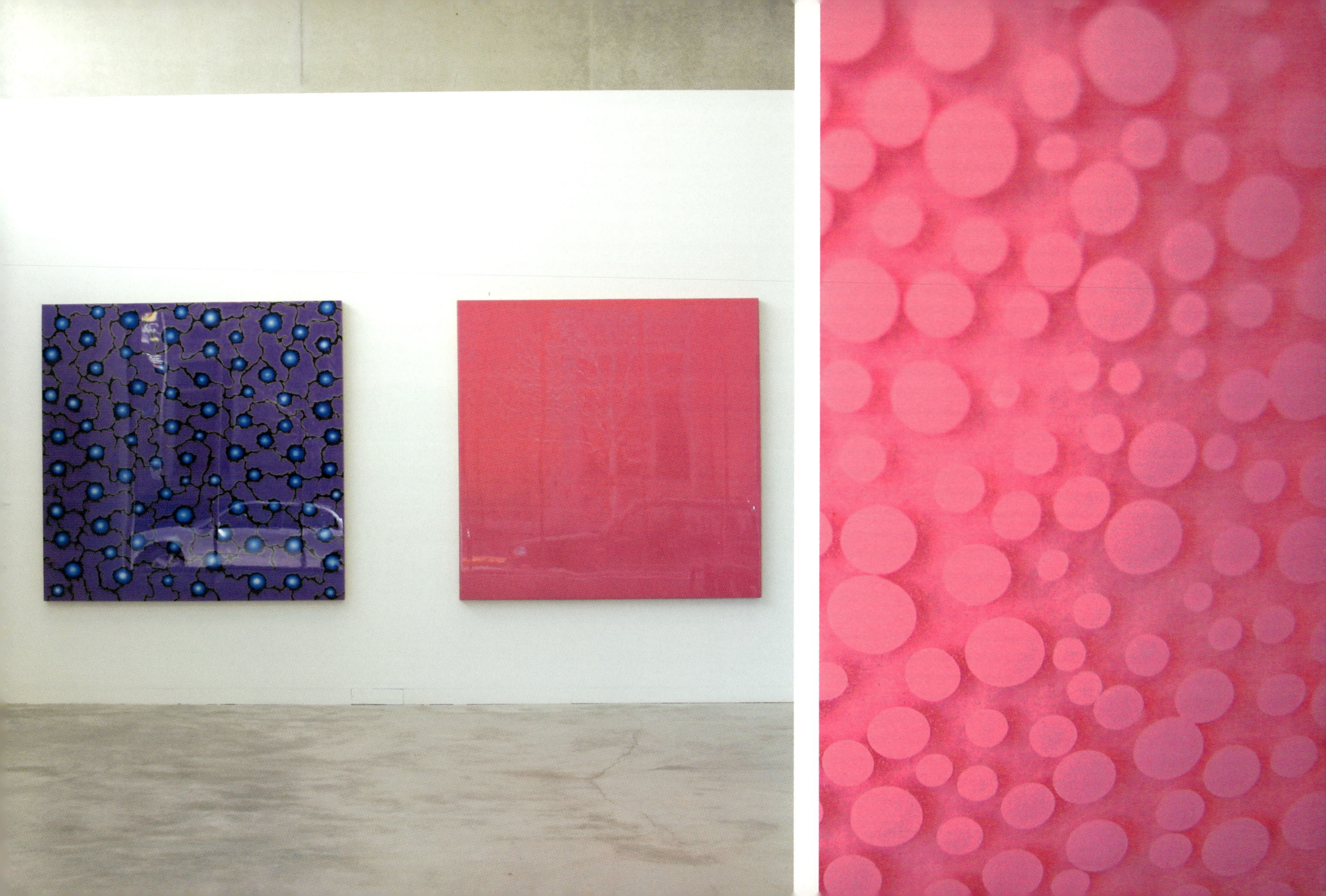

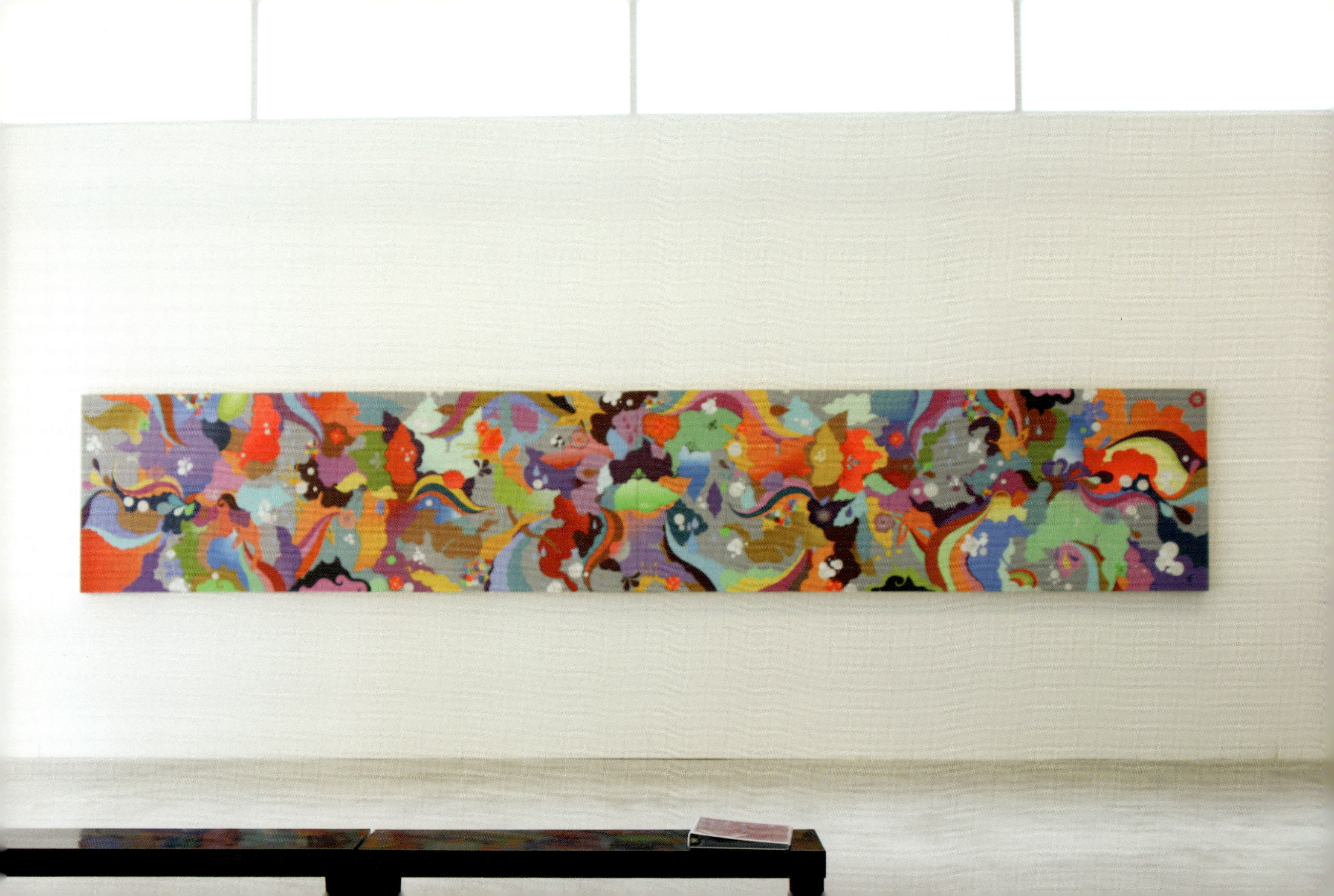

Soaring yet hypnotic, soft shapes and playful lines hold back the weight of an Easter palette milieu of colors. Similar to a cathedral stained glass window, the work sends a strong spiritual transmission. The work is coded with the entire history of art, but lives and disseminates information very much in the present – in the new stations of spirituality: museums, collections and clubs.[7]

Kandinsky believed the relationship between music and art to be the most profound and spiritual. Dzine's emotive works convey a joyful sense of spirituality through a visual longing and journey that is abstract but works to bring lofty aims down to earth. The installation *Punk Funk* is his most narrative work to date. Slightly off center is the core entrance into the work, which is literally through a wide-mouthed, vaginal-like opening flanked with beautifully rendered fallopian, fauna-filled tubes. This central work leads to a wavelike path that seems to beat in continuous motion towards some distant place--the Lost Kingdom? Perhaps. DJ Cam's title *The Lost Kingdom* further locates Dzine's new work in the realm of the narrative and the spiritual— wherein the utopian, the archaic, and the fantastic emerge in and out of focus and yet possess a sense of lightness in the now.

Yet Dzine's work reflects back on history and samples myriad cultural aesthetics as well. While the narrative component is structured much like a Hindu temple, which is also based on principles of the female body and birth, the work also makes reference to Persian Miniatures; Japanese woodblock prints and tattoo culture; Buddhist primordial mandala; Mexican Milagros (ex-voto's offered to saints); Nuyorican aesthetic borrowing; Art Nouveau Filigree; graffiti and air brush motorcycle work.

Dzine purposefully refers to his floating, glyph-like, jewel-colored motifs (highlighted in shimmering silver and gold) as offerings--gifts of spiritual importance or presents given in friendship and healing. His hovering ornaments are cultural gifts, miracles, and devotional charms that are rendered otherworldly and are made precious. In Tibetan Buddhism the mandala is an imaginary place that is contemplated during meditation. Dzine's Lost Kingdom could be inspired by this imaginary space that emerges in one's consciousness during moments of tranquility and peace. In his new work, the narrative enters the picture plane wherein each "floating" objects have unrevealed significance, perhaps representing some aspect of wisdom or reminding the viewer of some guiding principle.

While these specific cultural references may or may not surface for the viewer, they are nonetheless present in most of Dzine's work. Snippets of iconography and objects of various shapes, sizes, and colors are mixed together and become important to his abstract constructs. Dzine's work is sensual and organic. Curving lines and ornamentation fill his seductive paintings, reflecting acts of contemplation

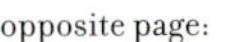

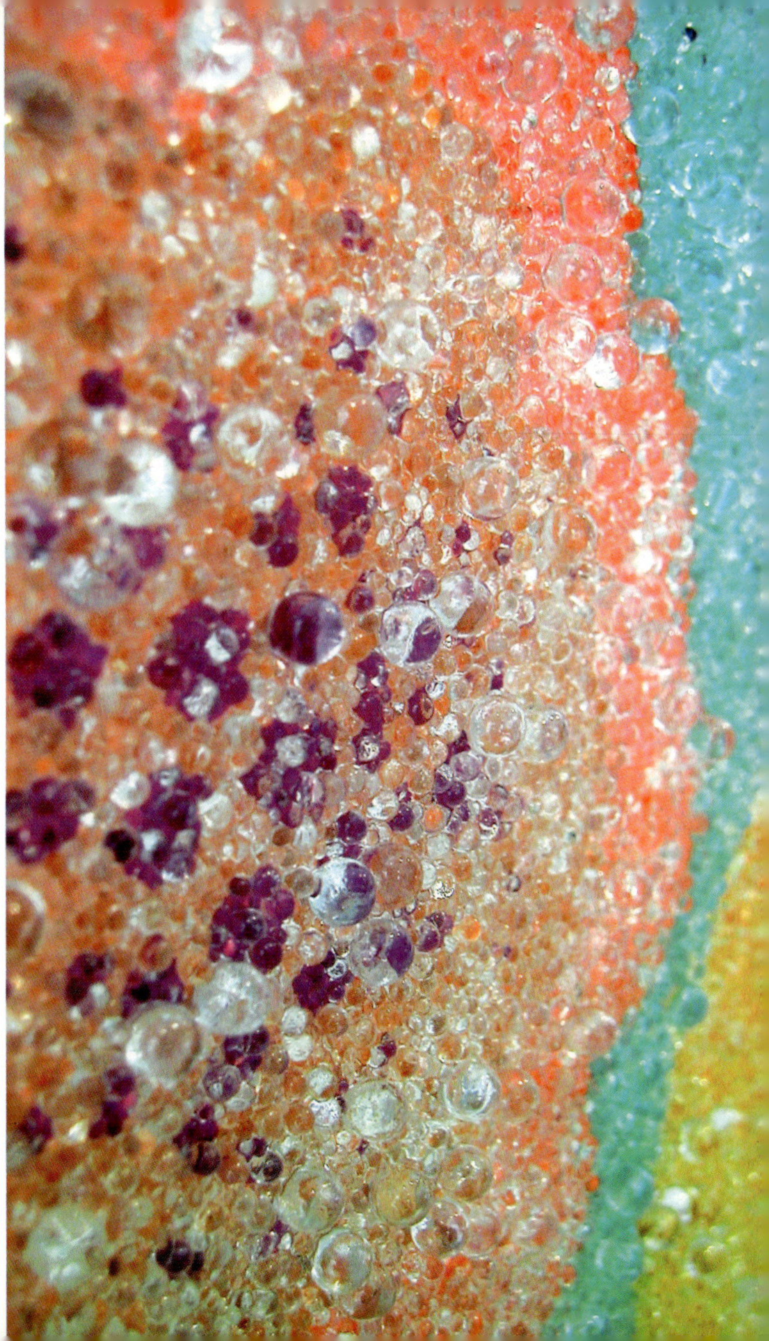

Love Junkee (detail), 2005, acrylic and glass beads on canvas on wood mount, (fabricated in collaboration with Maya Romanoff), 45 inches x 20 feet. Courtesy of the artist, Monique Meloche Gallery, Chicago, SCAI the Bathhouse/Shiraishi Contemporary Art Inc., Tokyo, and realized with the assistance of Contemporary Art Museum St. Louis. Photo: Blyth Renate Meier.

opposite page:
Love Junkee, 2005, installation view at the Contemporary Art Museum St. Louis. Photo: Bruce Burton.

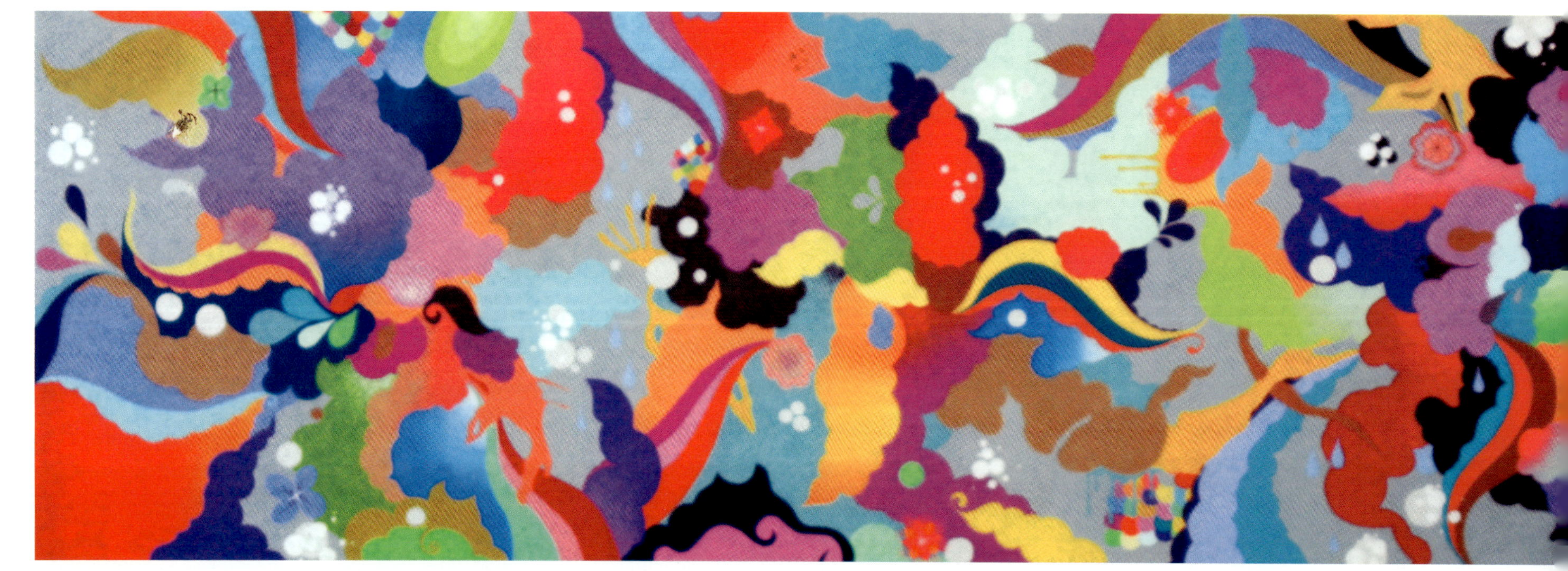

Love Junkee, 2005, acrylic and glass beads on canvas on wood mount, (fabricated in collaboration with Maya Romanoff), 45 inches x 21 feet. Courtesy of the artist, Monique Meloche Gallery, Chicago, SCAI the Bathhouse/Shiraishi Contemporary Art Inc., Tokyo, and realized with the assistance of Contemporary Art Museum St. Louis. Photo: Bruce Burton.

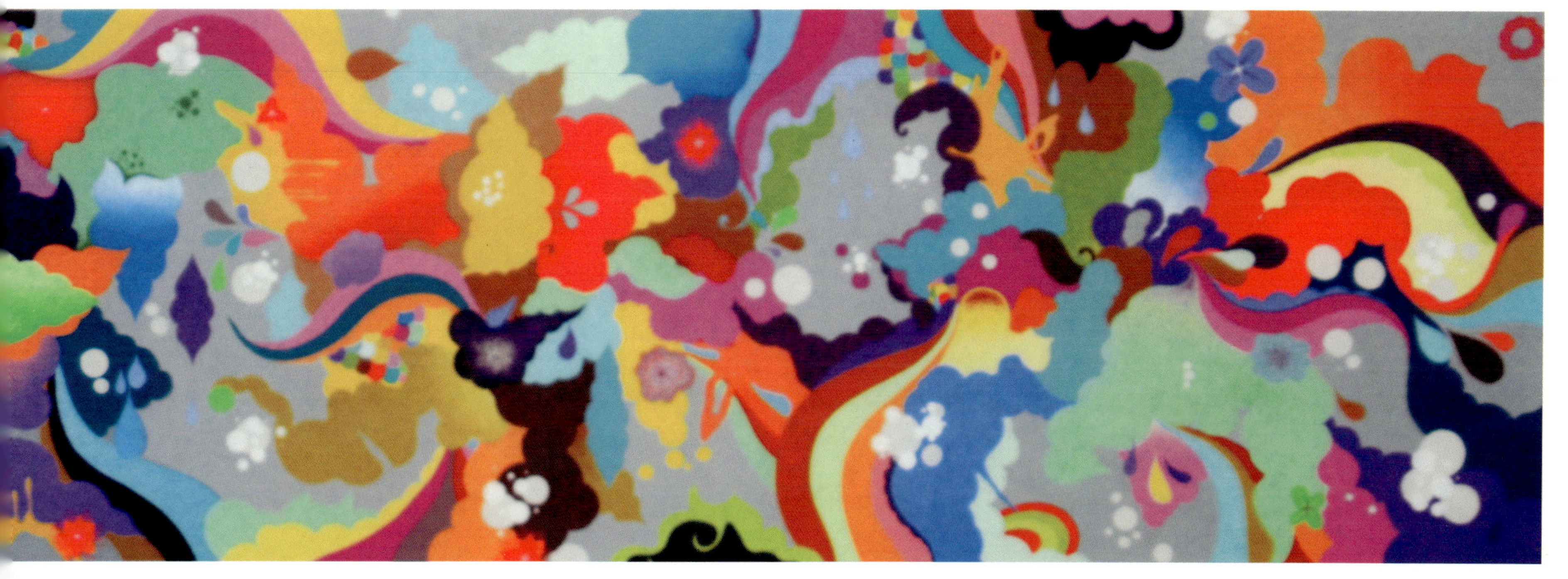

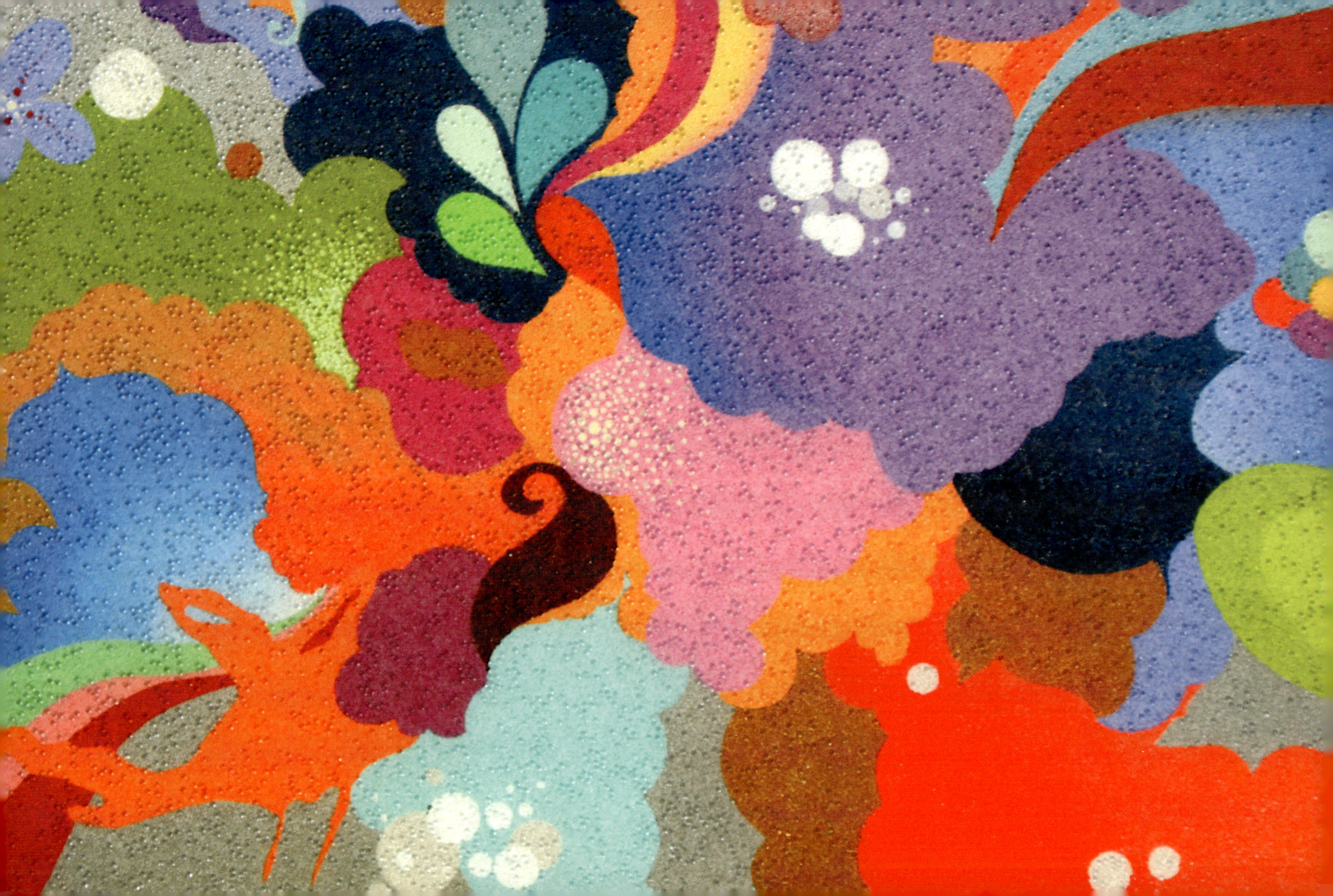

Il presente volume è stampato in 1000 copie / Printed in 1000 copies

Finito di stampare nel mese di aprile 2014
Printed April 2014

ISBN 9788836628698

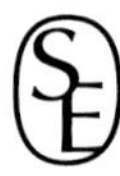

Silvana Editoriale
www.silvanaeditoriale.it

Direzione editoriale / Direction
Dario Cimorelli

Art Director
Giacomo Merli

Coordinamento organizzativo /
Production Coordinator
Michela Bramati

Segreteria di redazione / Editorial Assistant
Emma Altomare

Ufficio iconografico / Photo Editor
Alessandra Olivari, Silvia Sala

Ufficio stampa / Press Office
Lidia Masolini, press@silvanaeditoriale.it

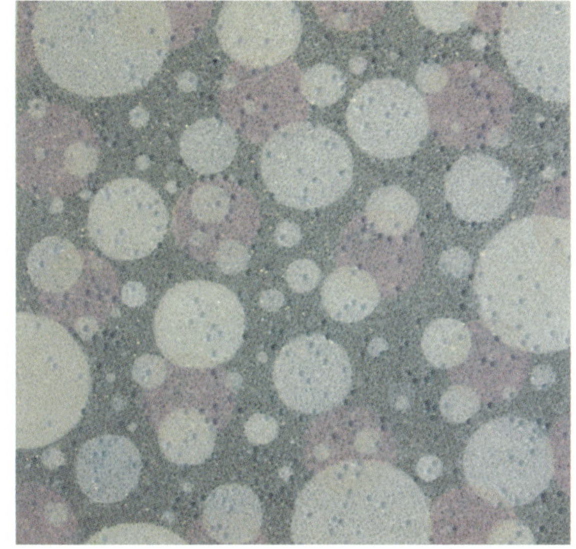 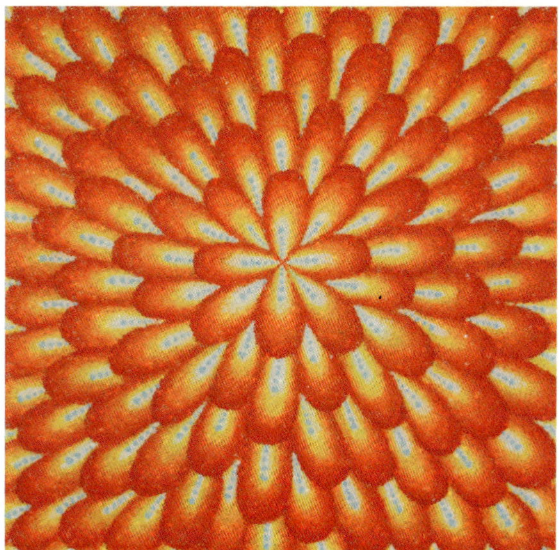 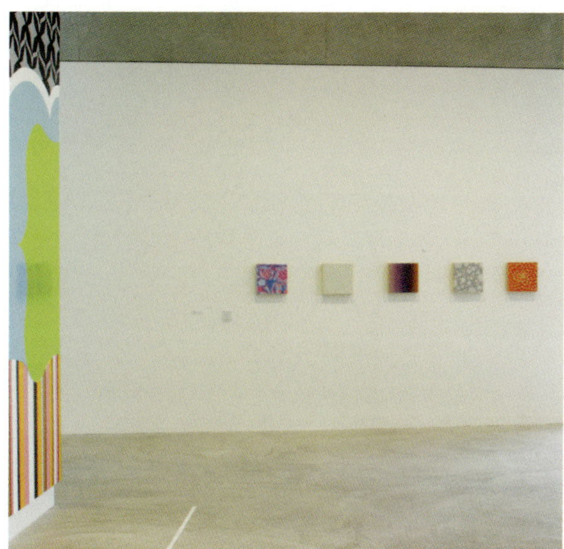

left to right:
Untitled from the Optick Interlude Series, 2004, acrylic and glass beads on wood mount, (fabricated in collaboration with Maya Romanoff), 12 x 12 inches. Collection of Andrew and Mary Ann Srenco, St. Louis. Photo: Bruce Burton.
Untitled from the Optick Interlude Series, 2005, acrylic and glass beads on wood mount, (fabricated in collaboration with Maya Romanoff), 12 x 12 inches. Collection of Sara Szold, Chicago. Photo: Bruce Burton.
Punk Funk, 2005, installation view at the Contemporary Art Museum St. Louis. Photo: Bruce Burton.

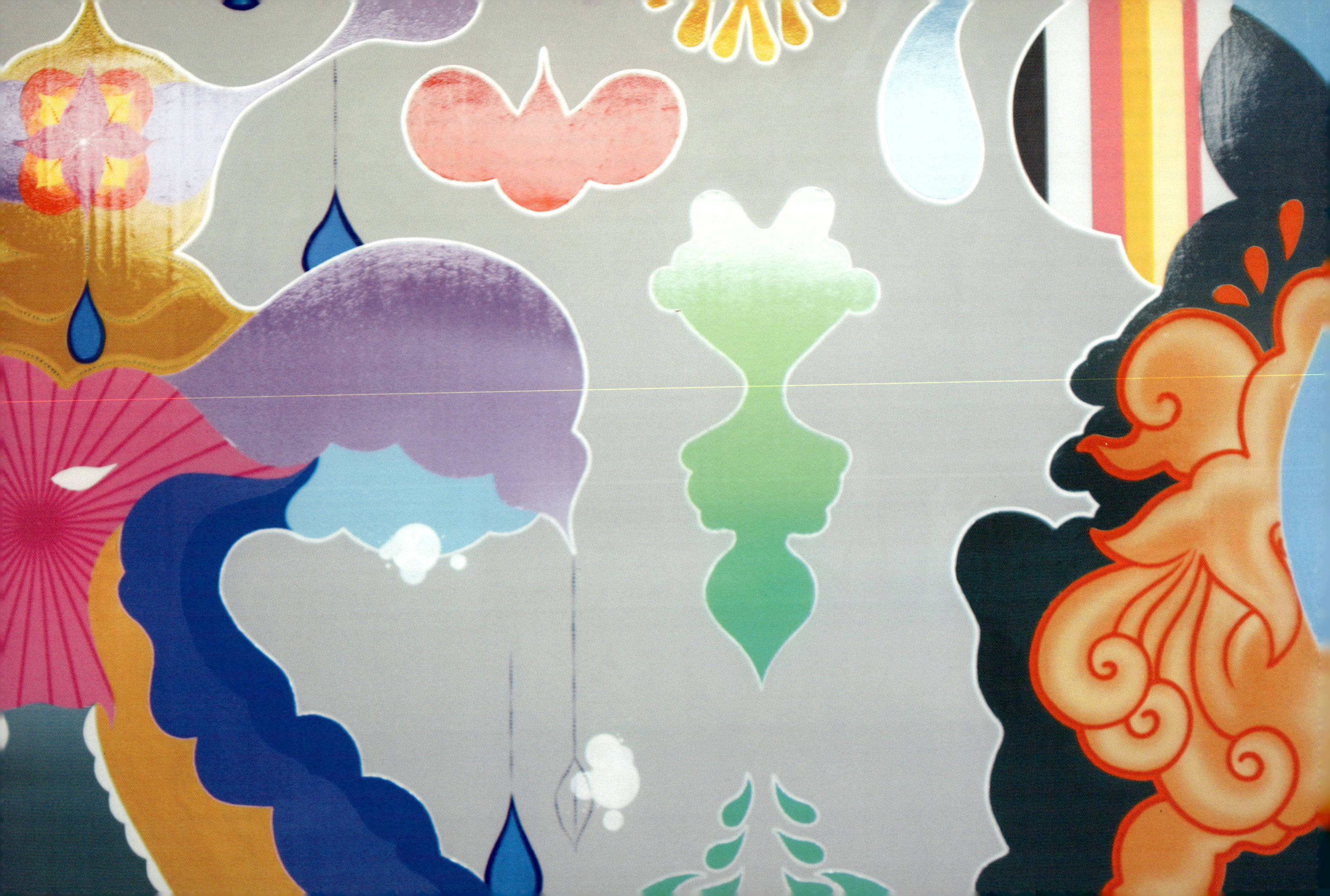

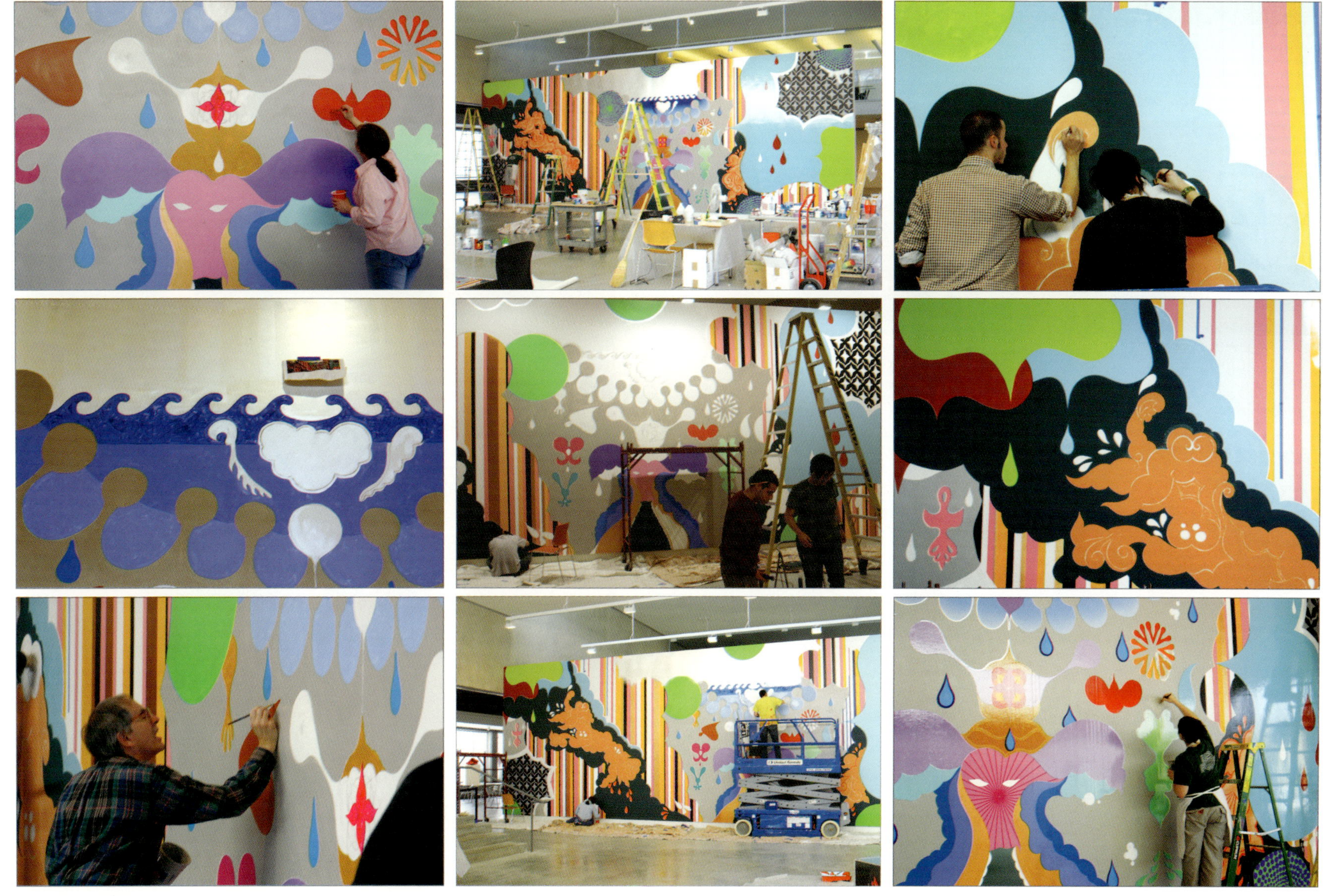

Punk Funk (installation views), 2005. Contemporary Art Museum St. Louis. Photo: Bruce Burton.

opposite page:
Punk Funk (detail), 2005. Contemporary Art Museum St. Louis. Photo: Bruce Burton.

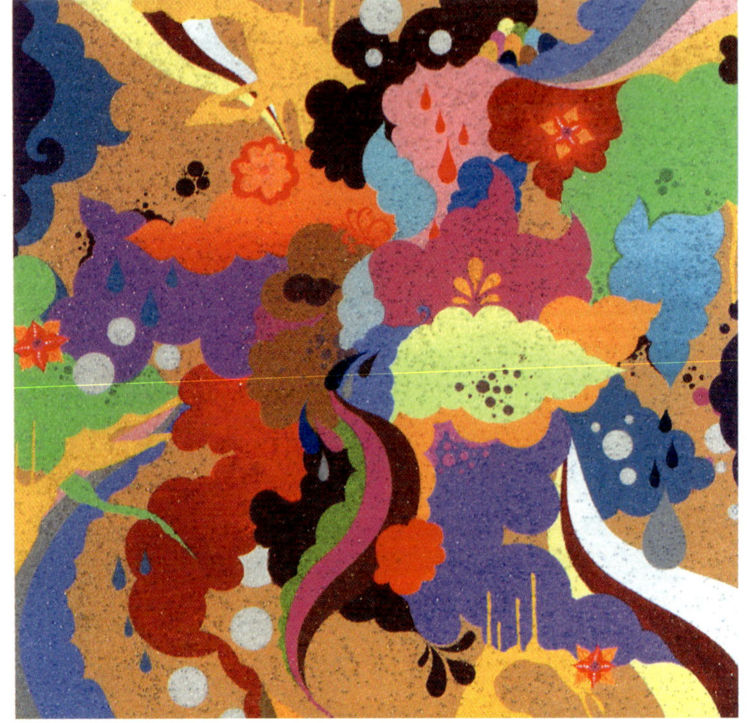

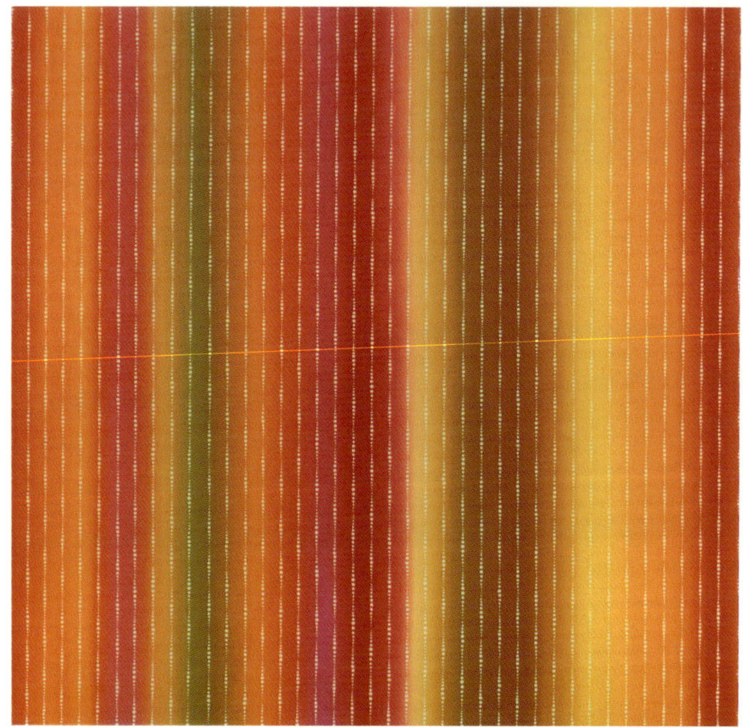

left to right:
Staring at the Sun, 2004, acrylic on canvas on wood mount with glass beads (fabricated in collaboration with Maya Romanoff), 40 x 40 inches. Collection of Marc & Liza Brooks, Chicago. Photo: Tom Van Eynde.
Stars and Ghosts, 2004, acrylic and envirotex on canvas on wood mount, 40 x 40 inches. Collection of Brian Muir, Chicago. Photo: Tom Van Eynde.

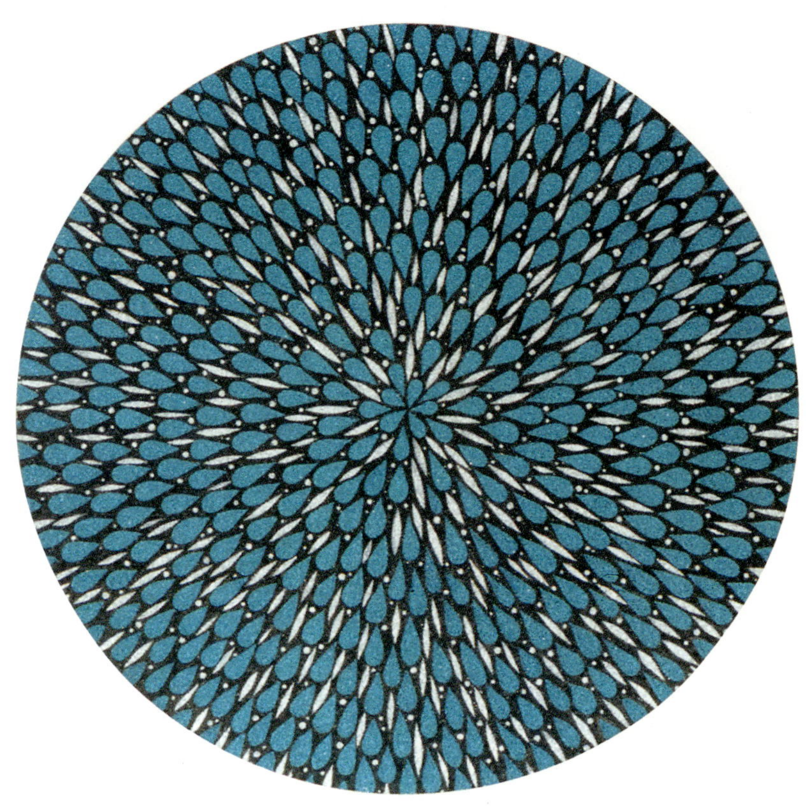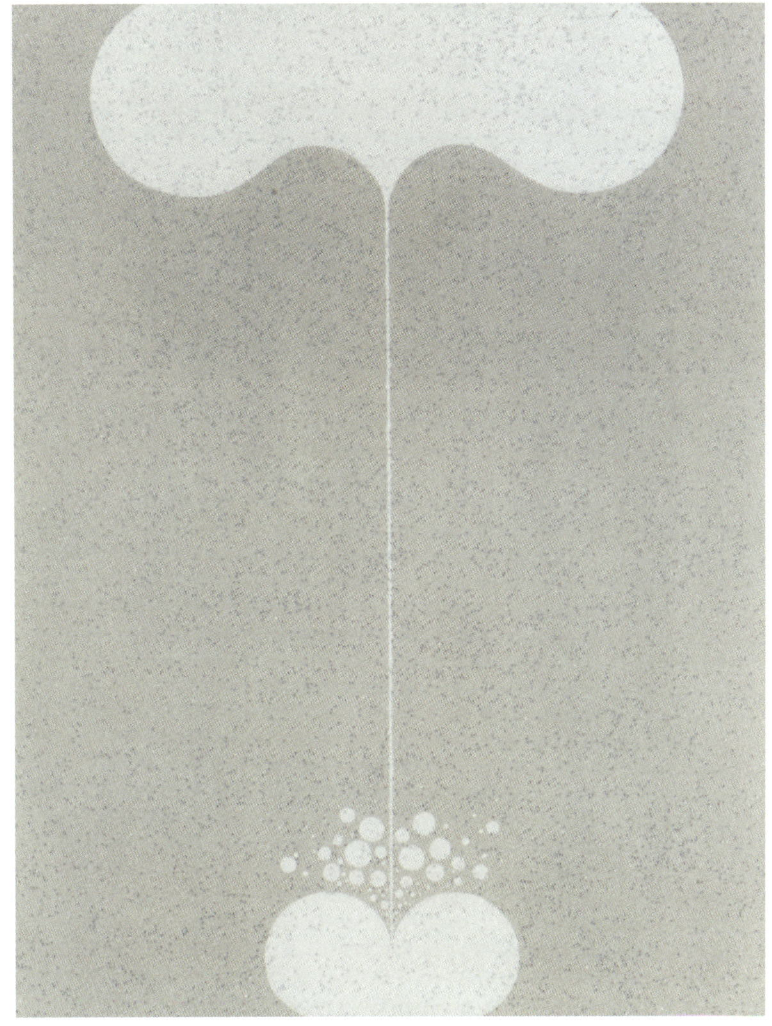

25

left to right:
People Pushing By, Walking Off Into the Light, 2004, acrylic on canvas on wood mount with glass beads (fabricated in collaboration with Maya Romanoff), 44 inch diameter. Collection of Mara & Javier Mendez, Puerto Rico.
Photo: Tom Van Eynde.
Diamond Studded, Pearl Necklace, 2004, acrylic on canvas on wood mount with glass beads (fabricated in collaboration with Maya Romanoff), 60 x 45 inches. Collection of Mark Vanmoerkerke, Belgium. Photo: Tom Van Eynde.

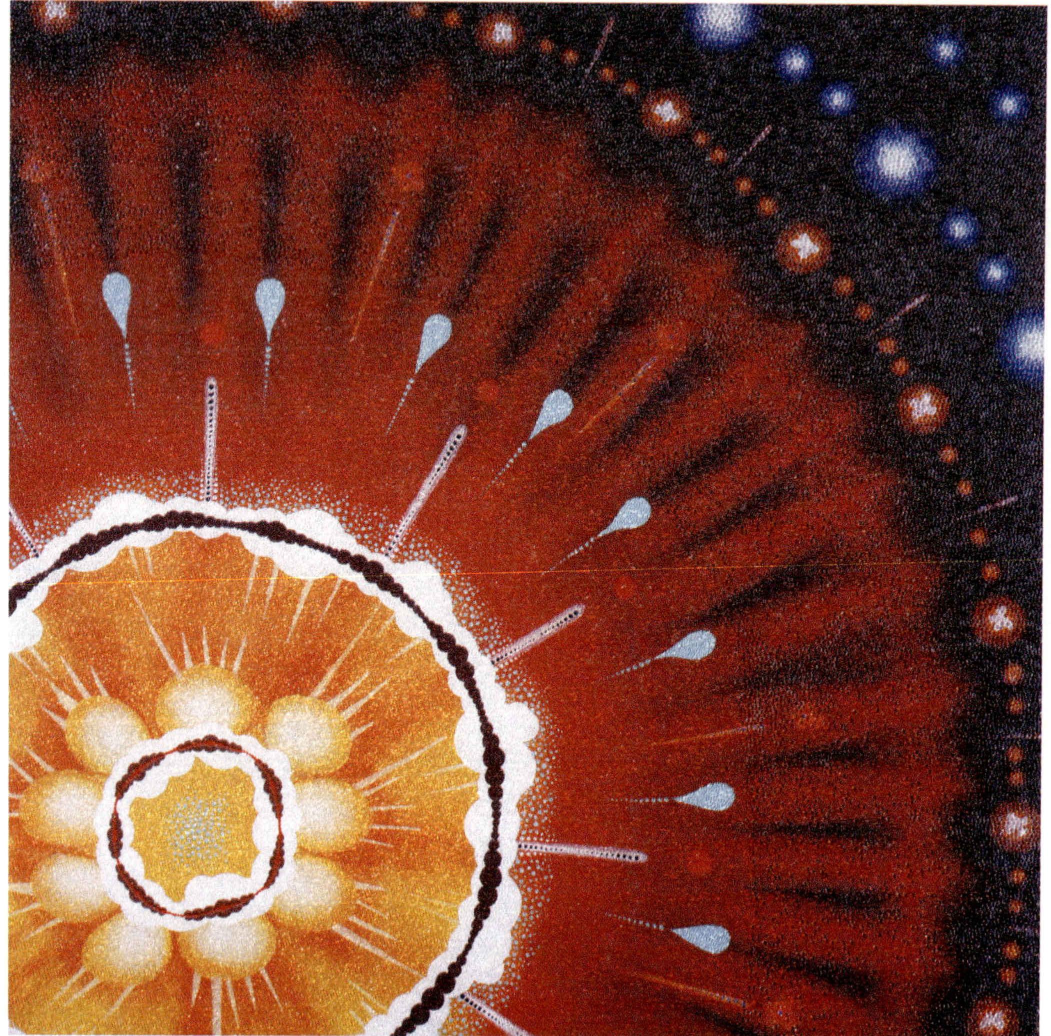

Bangkok Bazaar, 2005, acrylic on canvas on wood mount with glass beads (fabricated in collaboration with Maya Romanoff), 40 x 40 inches. Courtesy of the artist, Monique Meloche Gallery, Chicago, and SCAI the Bathhouse/Shiraishi Contemporary Art Inc., Tokyo. Collection of Mark Vanmoerkerke, Belgium.

opposite page:
Gangster Boogie, 2004, installation at BlackBlock/Palais de Tokyo, Paris. Photo: Masaya Kuroki.

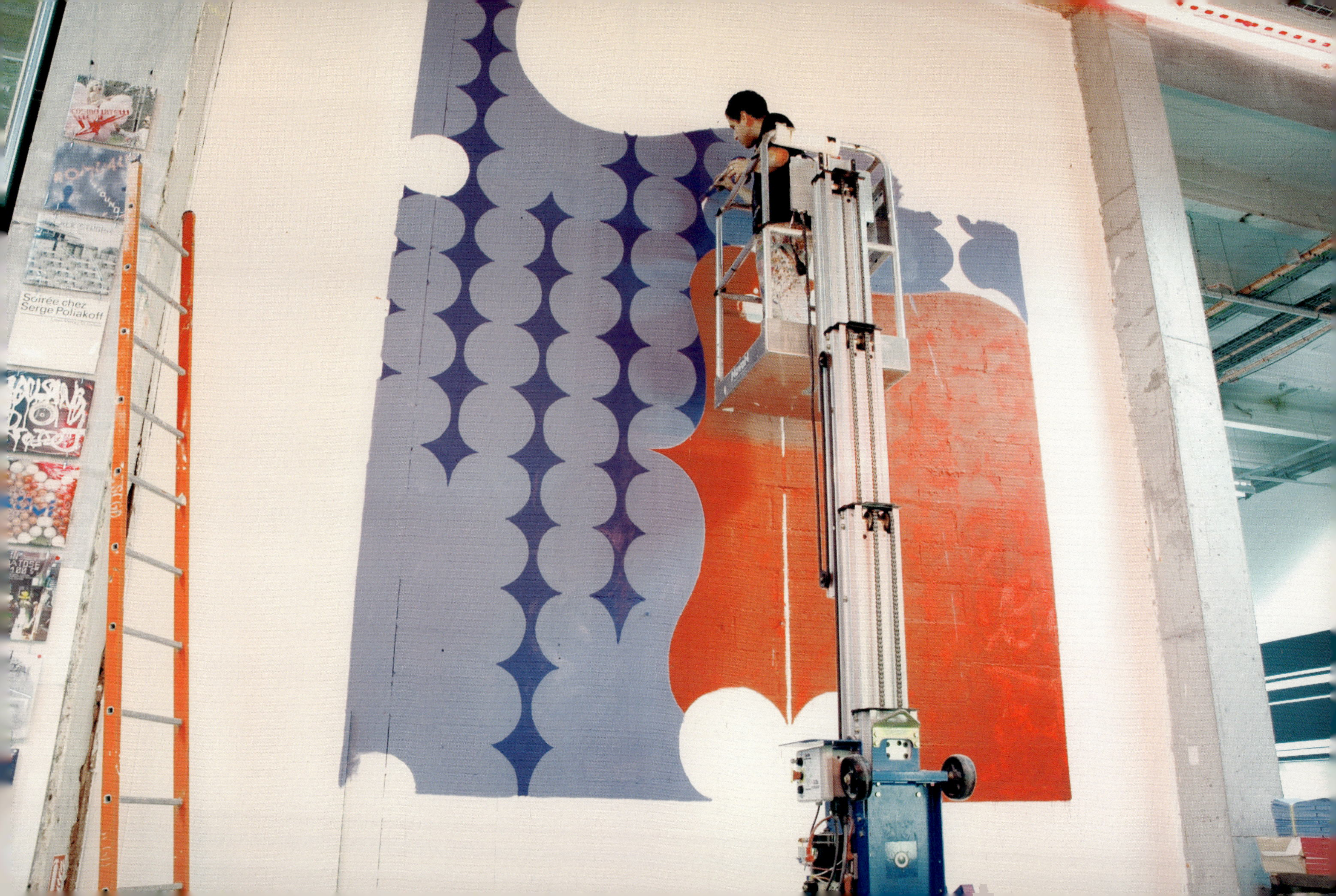

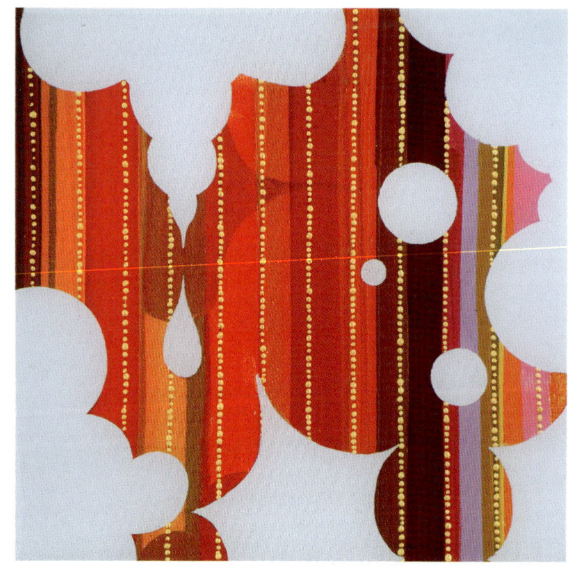 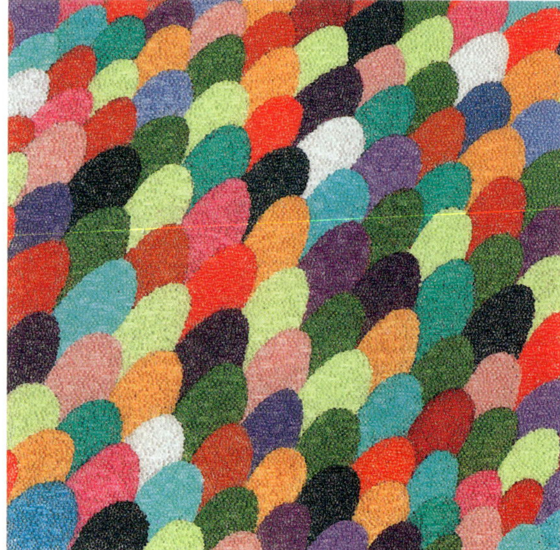 

left to right:
Study in Dub, 2004, acrylic and Envirotex on canvas on wood mount, 12 x 12 inches. Courtesy of Equal, Osaka and SCAI the Bathhouse/Shiraishi Contemporary Art Inc., Tokyo.
Untitled, 2004, acrylic on canvas on wood mount with glass beads (fabricated in collaboration with Maya Romanoff), 12 x 12 inches. Courtesy of Equal, Osaka and SCAI the Bathhouse/Shiraishi Contemporary Art Inc., Tokyo.
Getting Down with Daze, 2004, acrylic and Envirotex on canvas on wood mount, 12 x 12 inches. Courtesy of Equal, Osaka and SCAI the Bathhouse/Shiraishi Contemporary Art Inc., Tokyo.

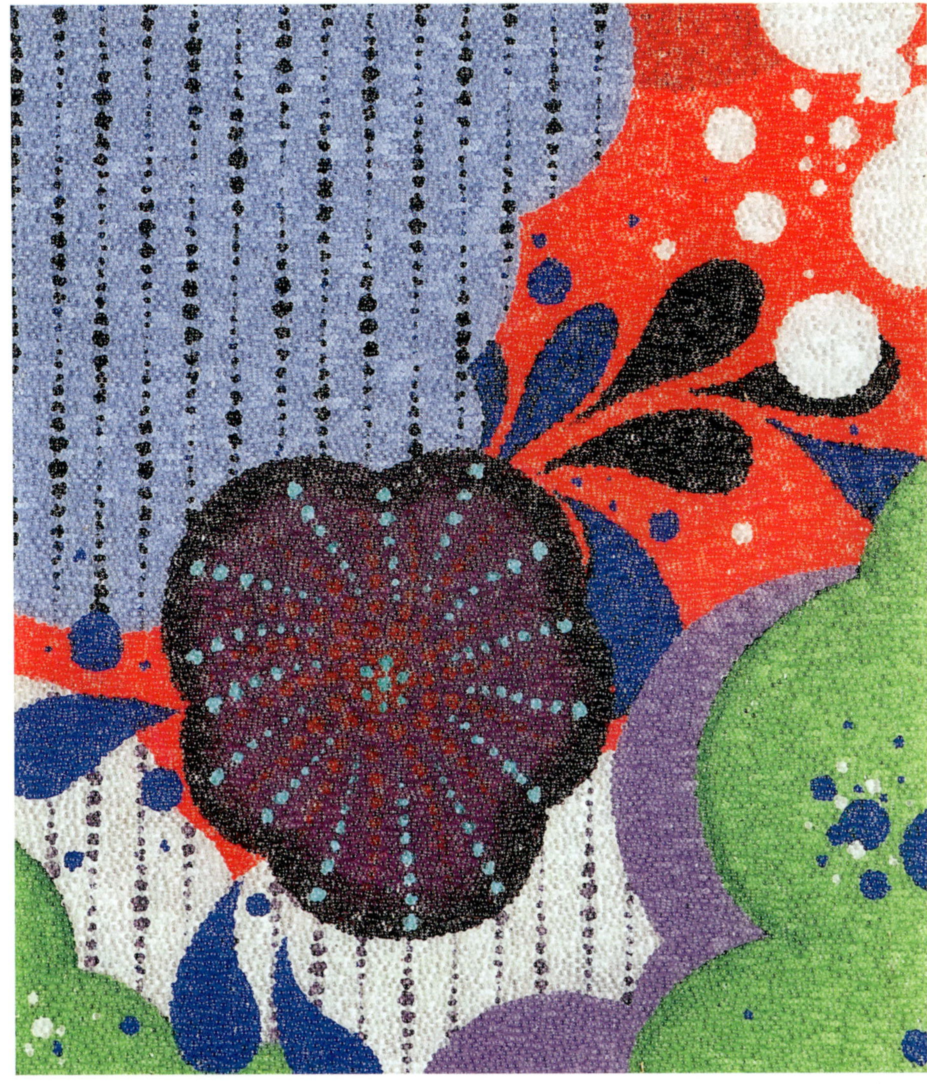

Study for Richest Man in Babylon 1, 2004, acrylic on canvas on wood mount with glass beads (fabricated in collaboration with Maya Romanoff), 10 x 12 inches.
Courtesy of Equal, Osaka and SCAI the Bathhouse/Shiraishi Contemporary Art Inc., Tokyo.

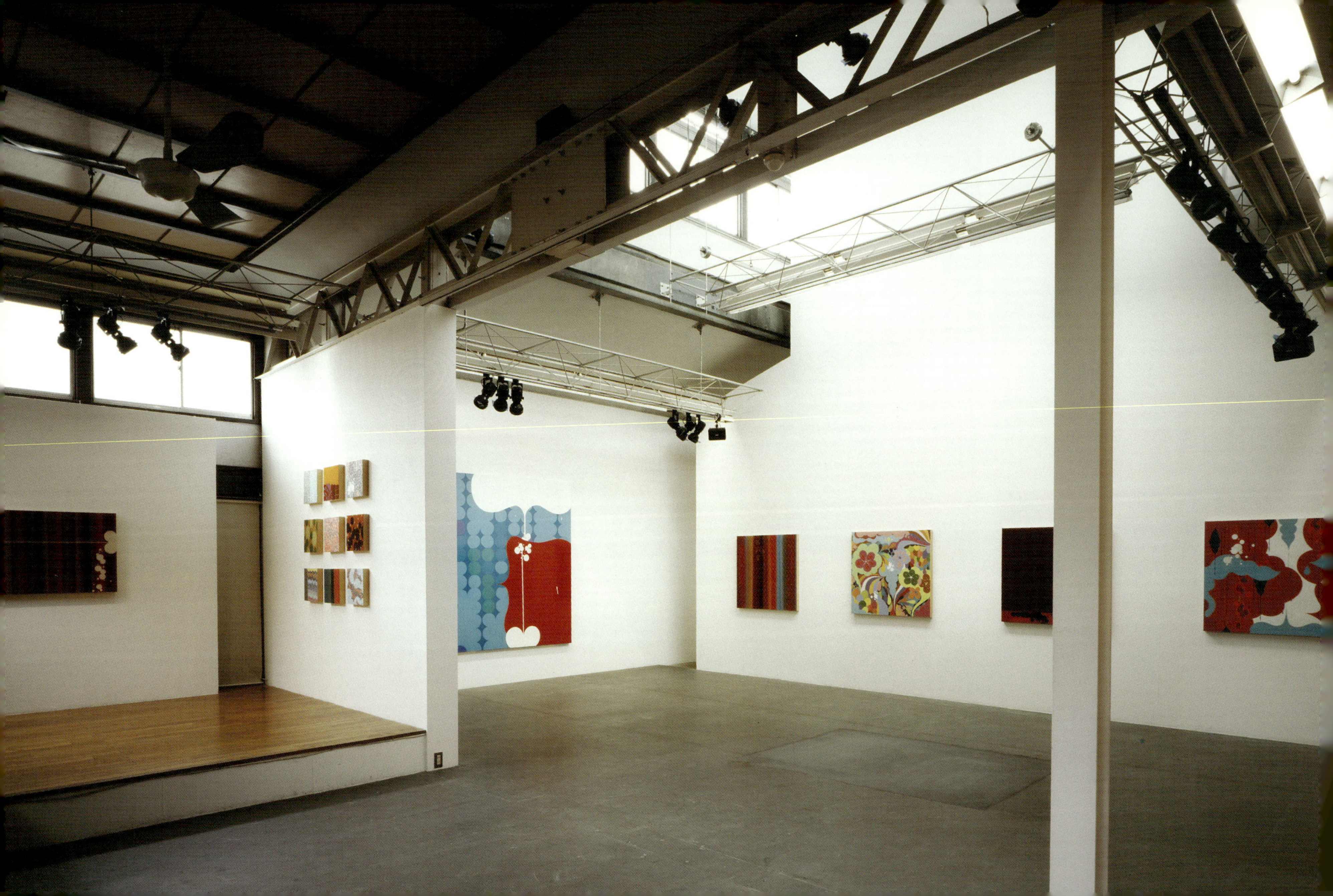

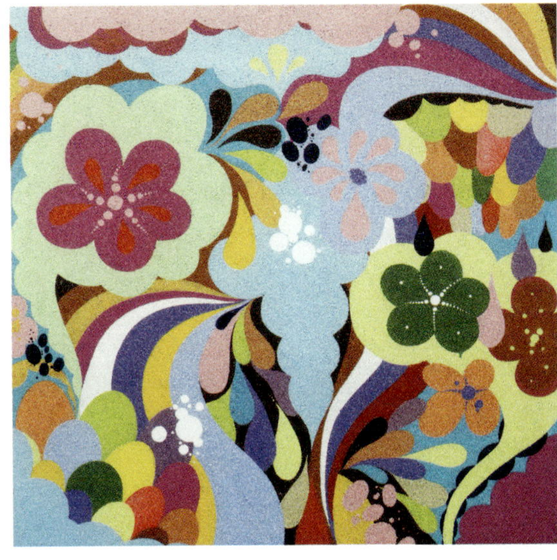 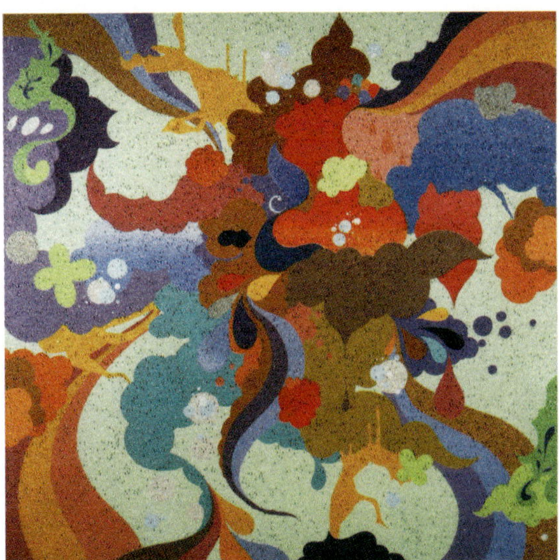 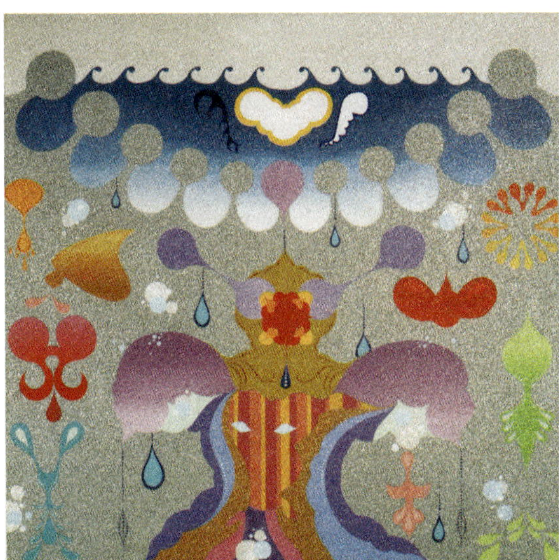

left to right:
The Richest Man in Babylon, 2004, acrylic on canvas on wood mount with glass beads (fabricated in collaboration with Maya Romanoff), 40 x 40 inches. Courtesy of SCAI the Bathhouse/Shiraishi Contemporary Art Inc., Tokyo.
Double Happiness, 2004, acrylic on canvas on wood mount with glass beads (fabricated in collaboration with Maya Romanoff), 40 x 40 inches. Courtesy of SCAI the Bathhouse/Shiraishi Contemporary Art Inc., Tokyo.
Pleasure Below, 2004, acrylic on canvas on wood mount with glass beads (fabricated in collaboration with Maya Romanoff), 40 x 40 inches. Courtesy of SCAI the Bathhouse/Shiraishi Contemporary Art Inc., Tokyo.

opposite page:
Beautiful Things, 2004, installation view at SCAI the Bathhouse/Shiraishi Contemporary Art Inc., Tokyo. Courtesy of SCAI the Bathhouse/Shiraishi Contemporary Art Inc., Tokyo.

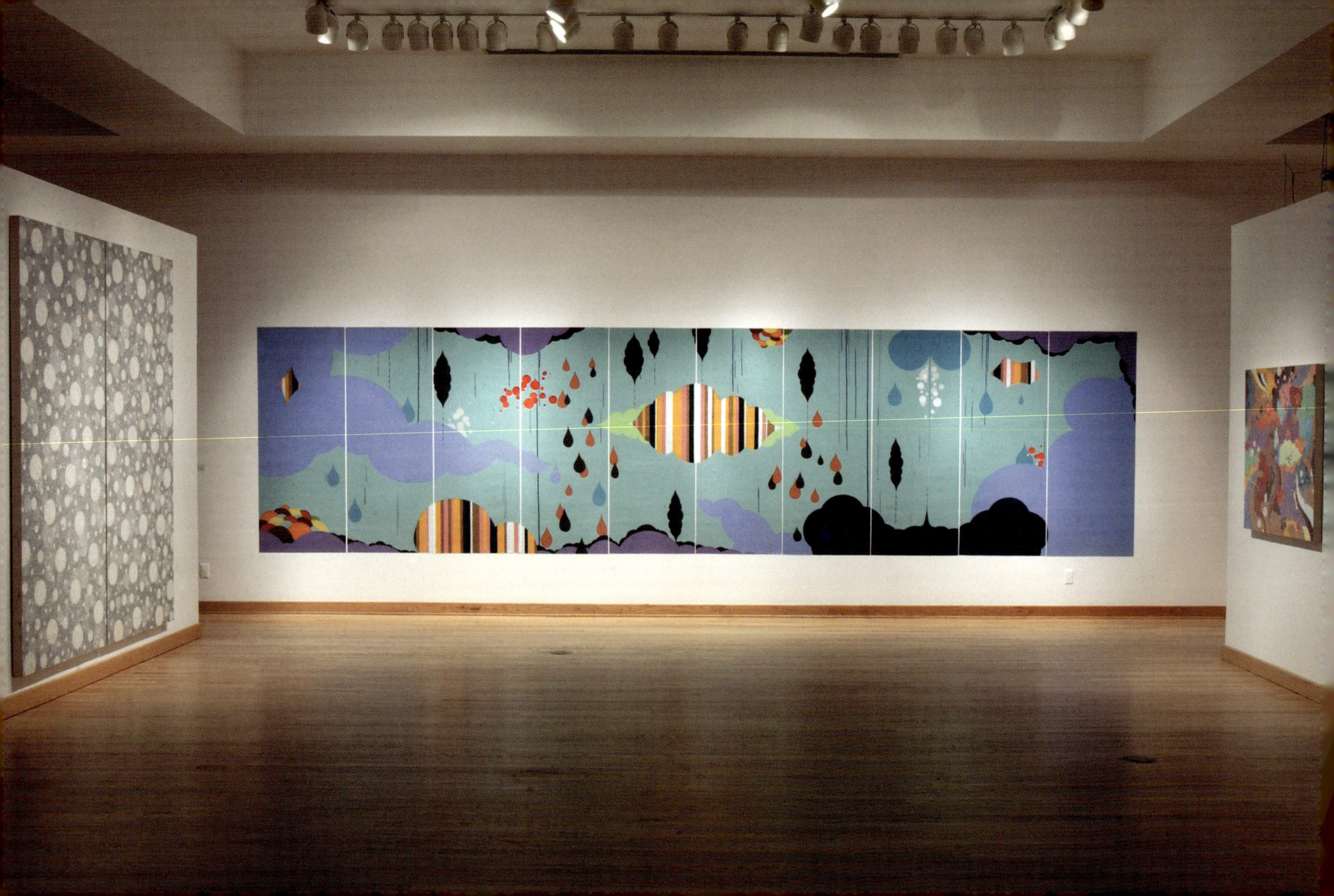

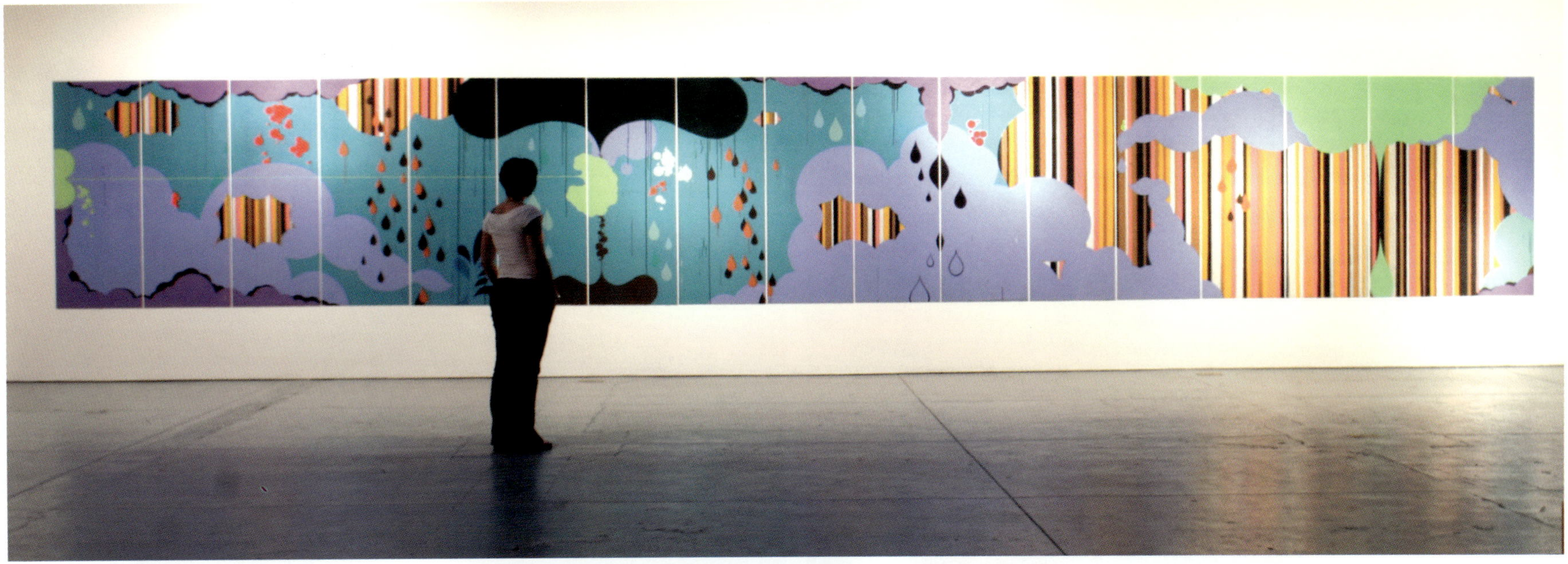

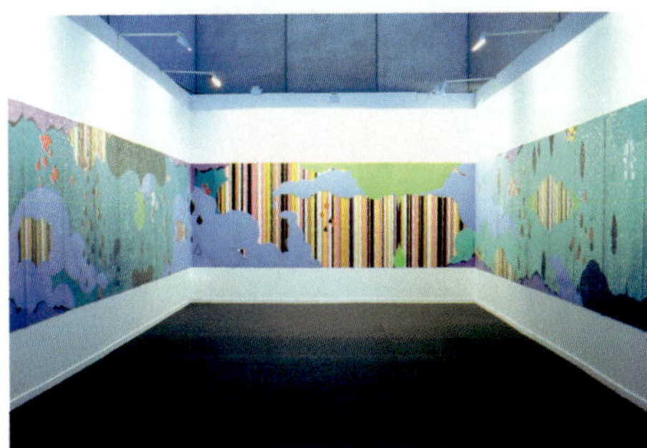 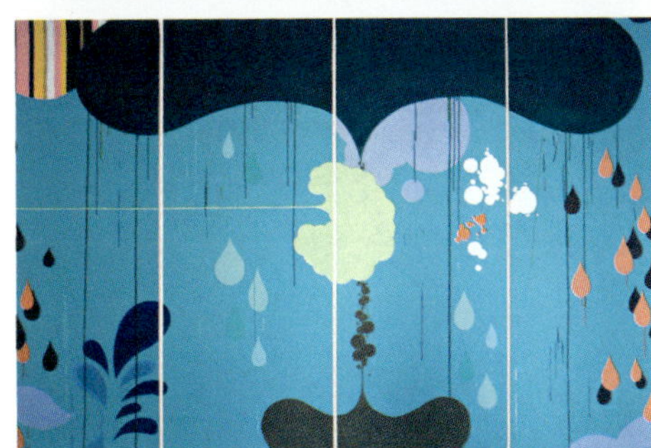 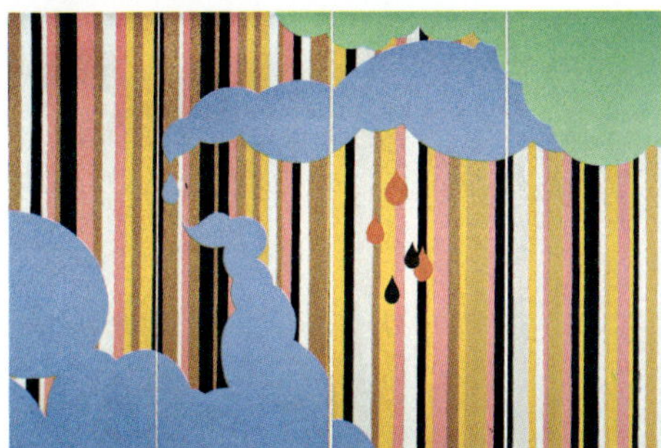

Beautiful Otherness, 2004 acrylic on canvas with glass beads (fabricated in collaboration with Maya Romanoff) installation view at Real Art Ways, Hartford, CT from exhibition "None of the Above: Contemporary Work by Puerto Rican Artists." Collection of Museo de Arte de Puerto Rico, San Juan. Promised Gift of SunCom Wireless. Photo: John Groo

Beautiful Otherness, 2004, acrylic on canvas with glass beads (fabricated in collaboration with Maya Romanoff), site specific installation @ ARCO 2004, Madrid (moniquemeloche project room), 27 parts, each 72 x 28 in., (left 10 parts, 6 x 24 feet., middle 7 parts, 6 x 16 feet., right 10 parts, 6 x 24 feet.).

Beautiful Otherness (details).

opposite page:
Installation view of *Lost in Music* exhibition, 2005, JCCC Gallery/Nerman Museum of Contemporary Art, Overland Park, Kansas.
(on left) *Lavender Lust*, 2005, acrylic on canvas with glass beads on wood mount (fabricated in collaboration with Maya Romanoff), dimensions 84 x 102 inches. Collection of Joel and Vivian Porkorny, Chicago.
(center) *Beautiful Otherness*, 2004, acrylic on canvas with glass beads (fabricated in collaboration with Maya Romanoff), dimensions 6 x 24 feet. Courtesy of the artist and Monique Meloche Gallery, Chicago.
(right) *Staring at the Sun*, 2004, acrylic on canvas on wood mount with glass beads (fabricated in collaboration with Maya Romanoff), dimensions 40 x 40 inches. Collection of Marc and Liza Brooks, Chicago.

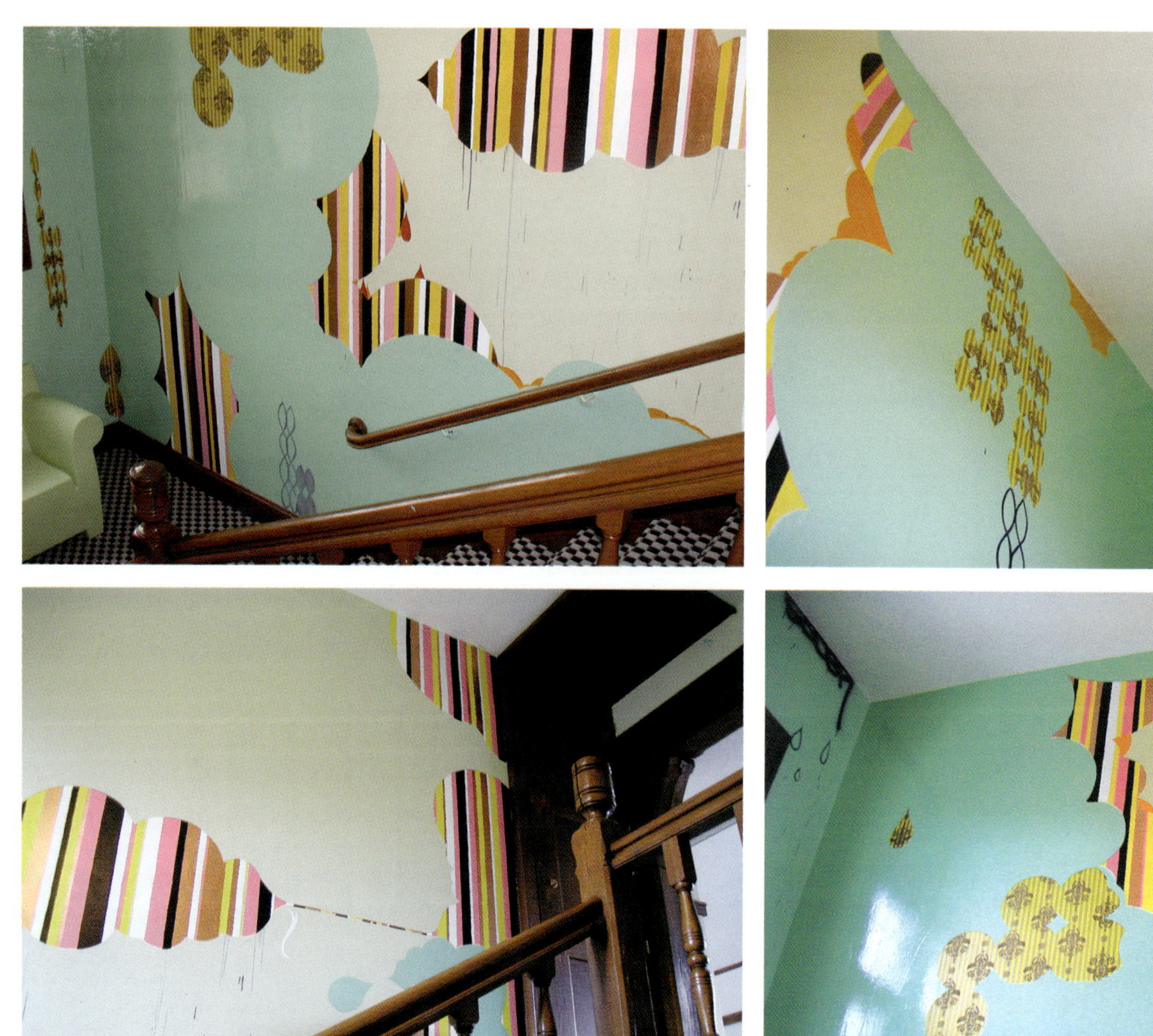

alley oop, 2003, acrylic, collage, and Envirotex on wall, site-specific installation, Institute of Visual Arts (INOVA), University of Wisconsin – Milwaukee, Wisconsin. Photos: Blyth Renate Meier.

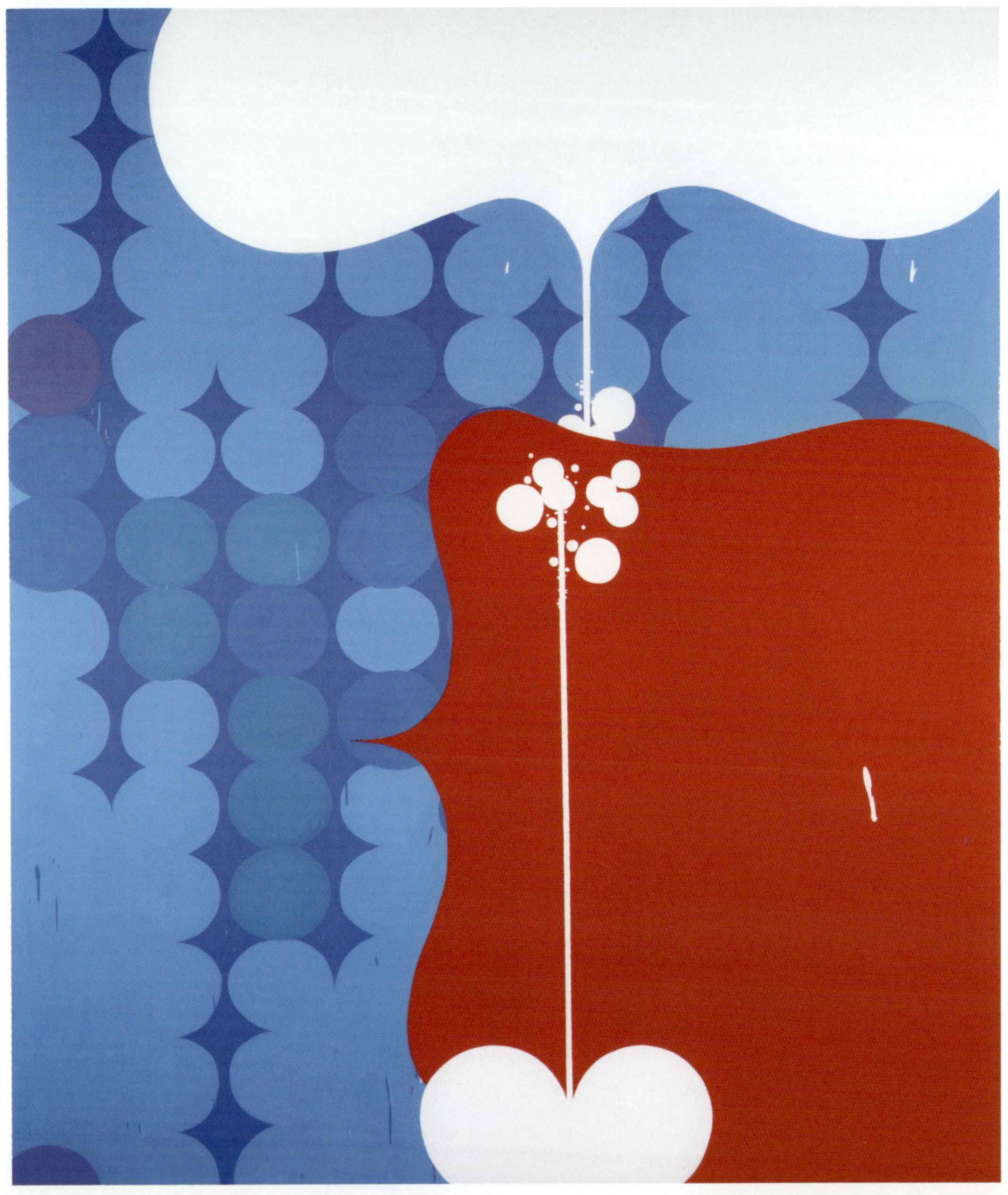

Gangster Boogie, 2002, acrylic and Envirotex on canvas,
88 x 73 inches. Private Collection, Tokyo.

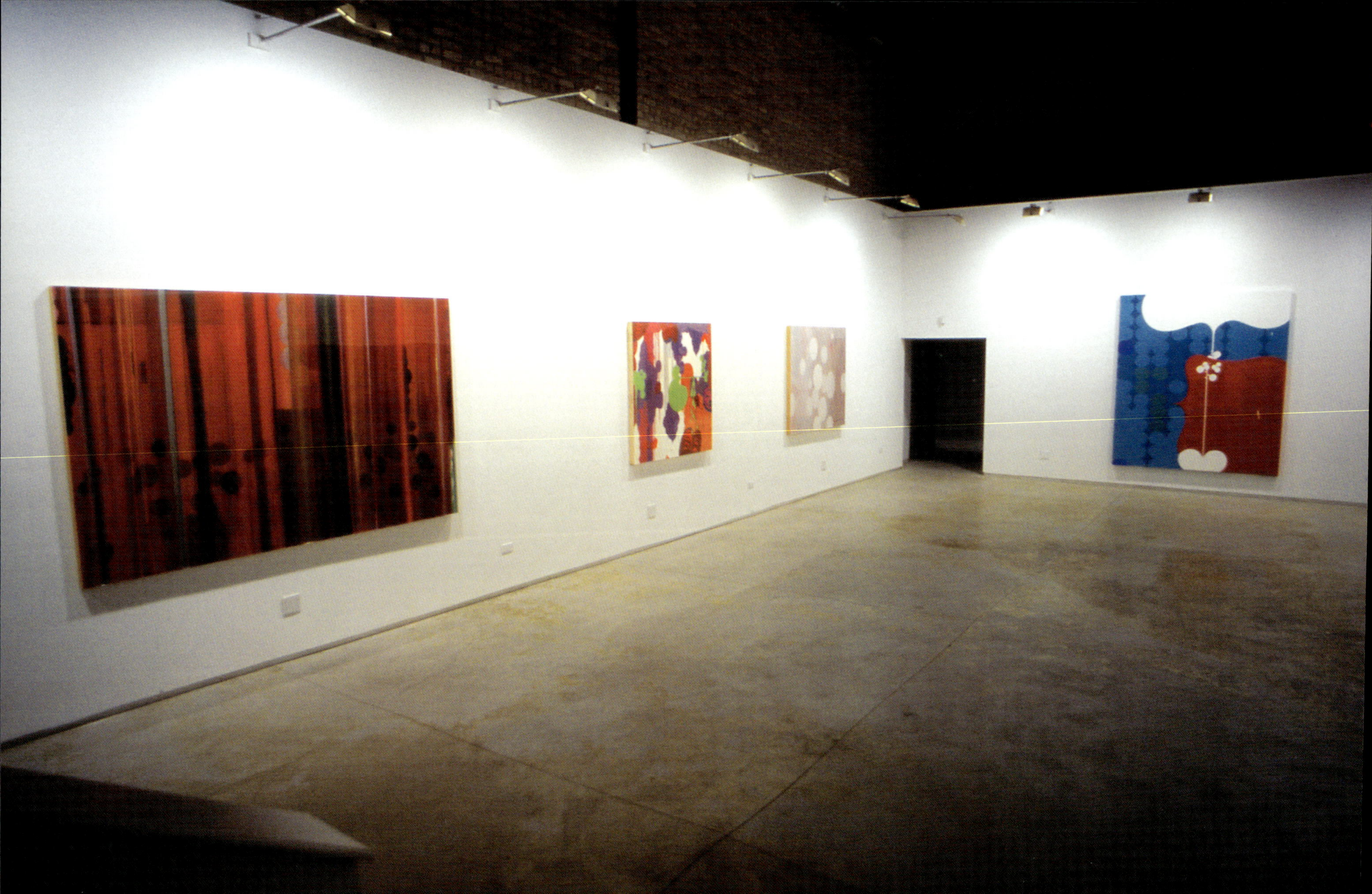

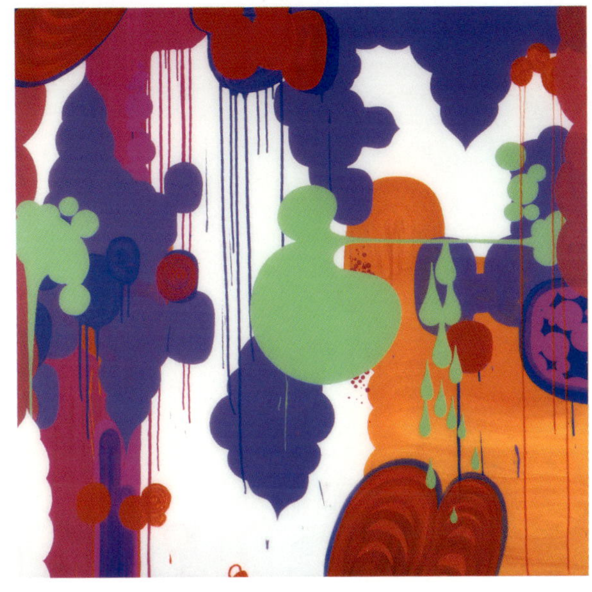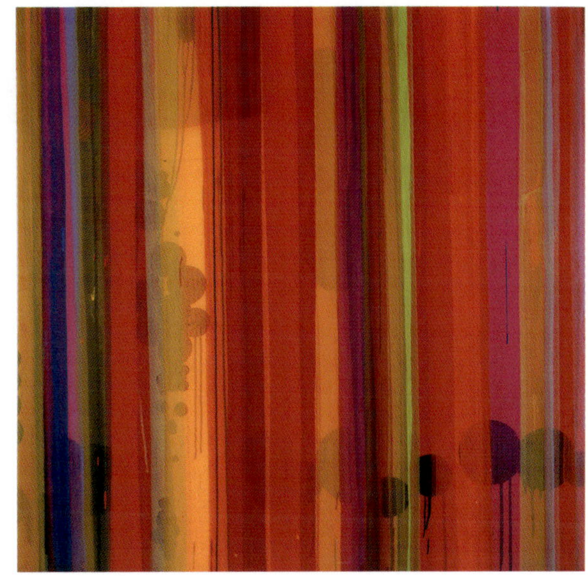

left to right:
bling, 2002, acrylic and Envirotex on canvas on wood mount, 50 x 50 inches. Collection of Abe Tomas Hughes, Highland Park, IL.
Rocksteady, 2002, acrylic, spray enamel, and Envirotex on canvas on wood mount, 50 x 50 inches. Collection of Douglas Van Putten, Chicago.

opposite page:
beat junkie, chop shop (installation view), 2002, solo exhibition at Monique Meloche Gallery, Chicago. Photo: Chris Strong.

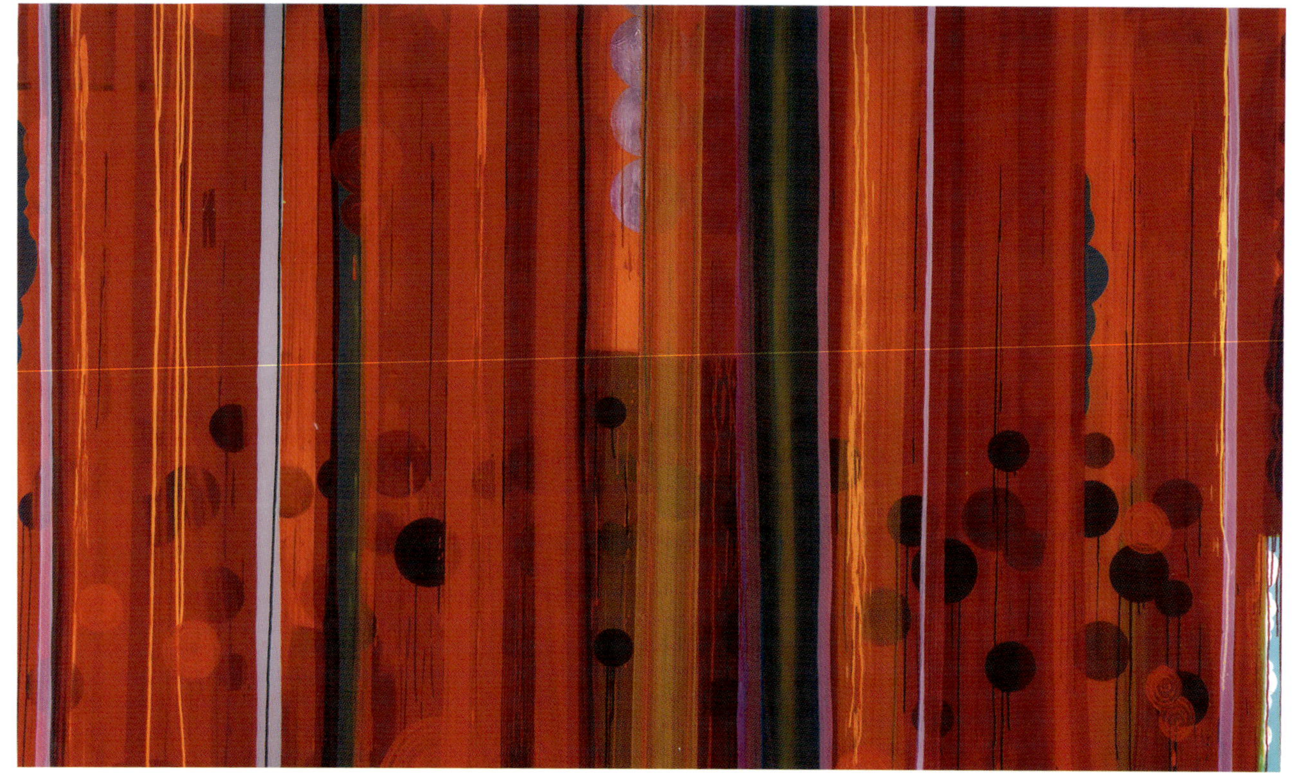

Zero 7, 2001-2002, acrylic and Envirotex on canvas on wood mount, 61 x 99 inches. Collection of Julie and Jamie Bellanca, Chicago.

opposite page:
sampler, 2002, acrylic, spay enamel and Envirotex on plywood, 8 x 30 feet., site specific installation at Museum of Contemporary Art, Chicago. Private Collection, Tokyo.

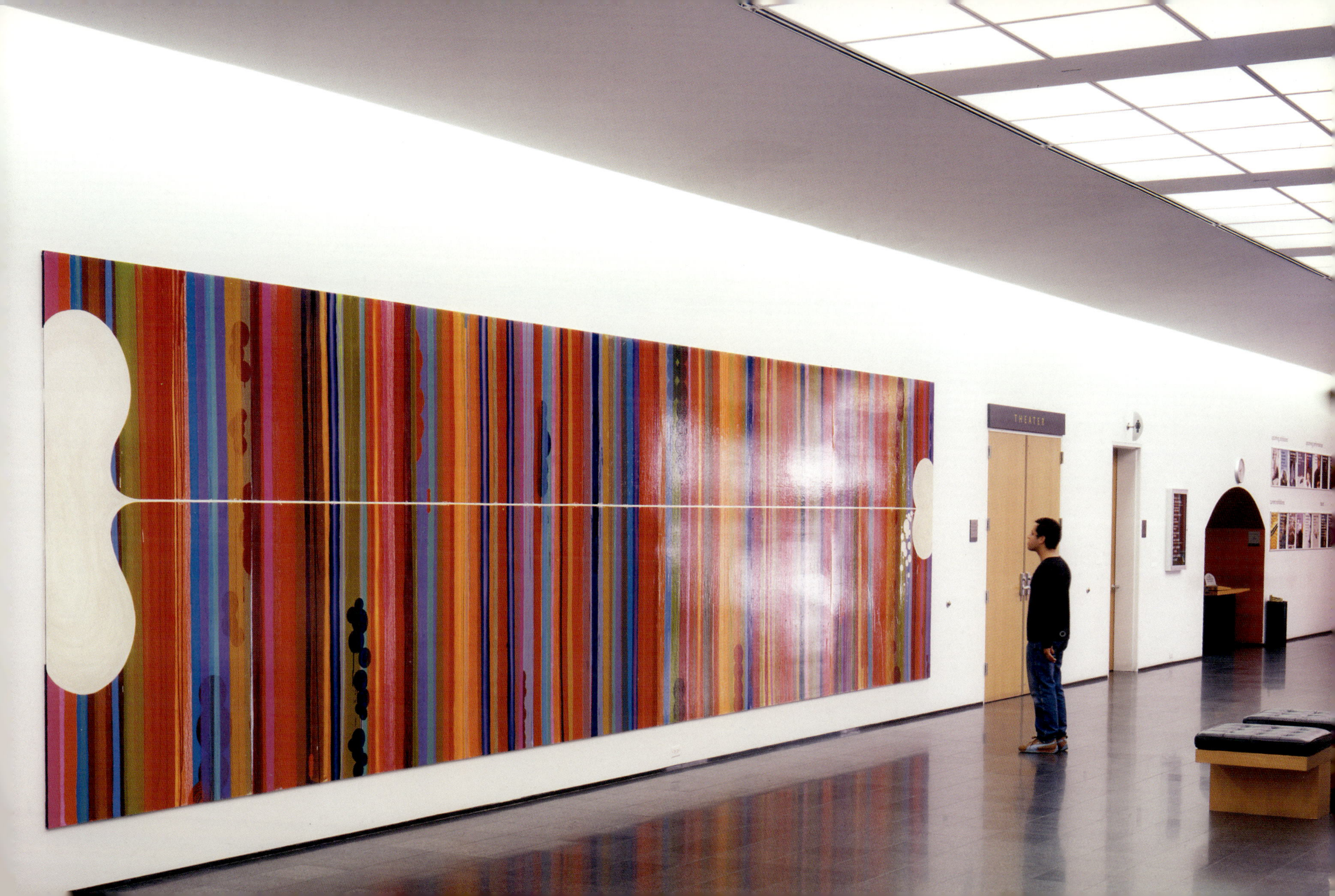

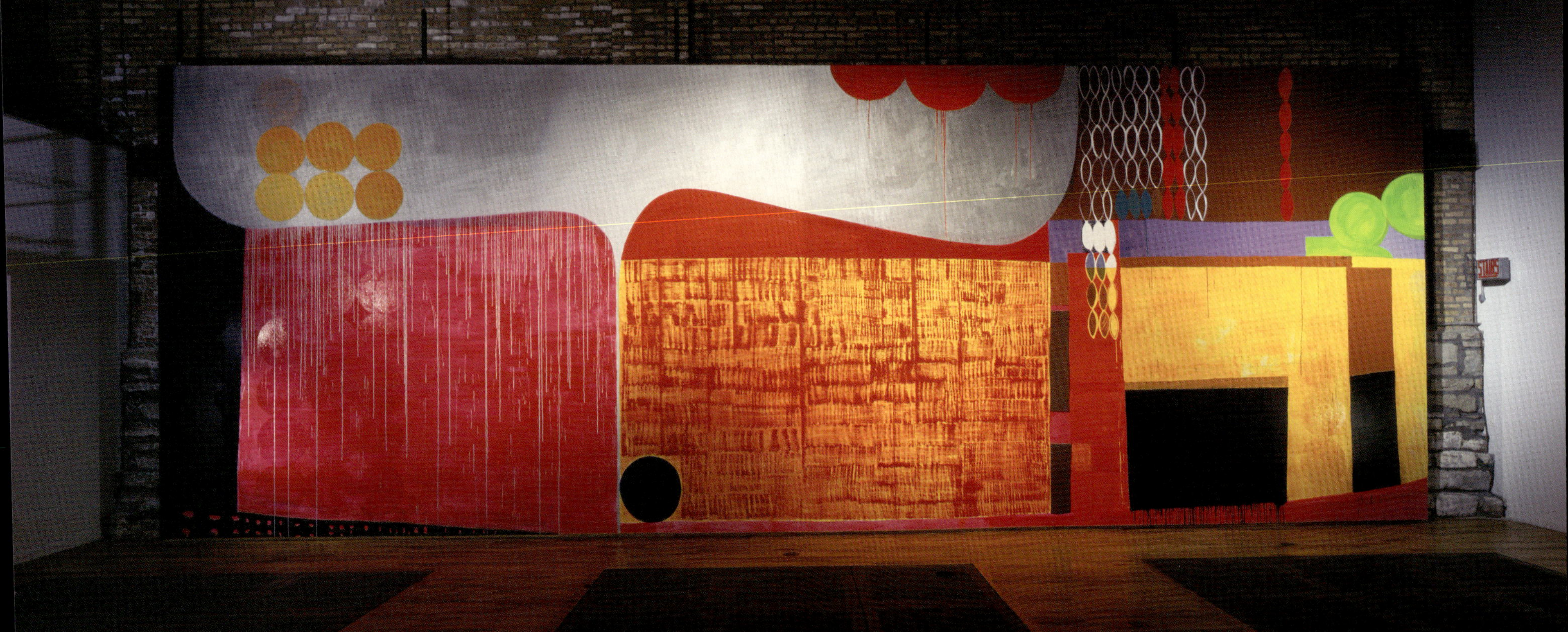

Exhibition Checklist

Punk Funk, 2005, acrylic, Envirotex, and varnish on wood mount attached to wall, 14 x 42 feet. Courtesy of the artist, Monique Meloche Gallery, Chicago, SCAI the Bathhouse/Shiraishi Contemporary Art Inc., Tokyo, and realized with the assistance of Contemporary Art Museum St. Louis.

Love Junkee, 2005, acrylic and glass beads on canvas on wood mount (fabricated in collaboration with Maya Romanoff), 45 inches x 21 feet. Courtesy of the artist, Monique Meloche Gallery, Chicago, SCAI the Bathhouse/Shiraishi Contemporary Art Inc., Tokyo, and realized with the assistance of Contemporary Art Museum St. Louis.

To be Continued, 2005, acrylic and Envirotex on canvas on wood mount, 70 x 70 inches. Courtesy of the artist, Monique Meloche Gallery, Chicago, SCAI the Bathhouse/Shiraishi Contemporary Art Inc., Tokyo, and realized with the assistance of Contemporary Art Museum St. Louis.

Friends and Enemies, 2005, acrylic and Envirotex on canvas on wood mount, 70 x 70 inches. Courtesy of the artist, Monique Meloche Gallery, Chicago, and SCAI the Bathhouse/Shiraishi Contemporary Art Inc., Tokyo, and realized with the assistance of Contemporary Art Museum St. Louis.

Untitled from the Optick Interlude Series, 2005, acrylic and Envirotex on wood mount, 12 x 12 inches. Collection of Donald L. Bryant, Jr. Family Art Trust.

Untitled from the Optick Interlude Series, 2004, acrylic and glass beads on wood mount (fabricated in collaboration with Maya Romanoff), 12 x 12 inches. Collection of Sigrid and Jeffrey Brooks, St. Louis.

Untitled from the Optick Interlude Series, 2004, acrylic and Envirotex on wood mount, 12 x 12 inches. Collection of Donald L. Bryant, Jr. Family Art Trust.

Untitled from the Optick Interlude Series, 2004, acrylic and glass beads on wood mount (fabricated in collaboration with Maya Romanoff), 12 x 12 inches. Collection of Andrew and Mary Ann Srenco, St. Louis.

Untitled from the Optick Interlude Series, 2005, acrylic and glass beads on wood mount (fabricated in collaboration with Maya Romanoff), 12 x 12 inches. Collection of Sara Szold, Chicago.

opposite page:
Dzine/Judy Ledgerwood/DJ Cam, *Search for Love*, 2001, acrylic and Envirotex on wall. Site specific installation at Gallery 312, Chicago.

Dzine Biography

Born Carlos Rolon 1970, Chicago, Illinois.

Selected Solo Exhibitions:

2005   Dzine: *Punk Funk*, Contemporary Art Museum St. Louis, St. Louis.
Dzine: *beautiful otherness: a solo project by Dzine*, Illinois State Museum, Lockport,
IL and Gallery 210, University of Missouri St. Louis, St. Louis.

2004   *staring at the sun*, Monique Meloche Gallery, Chicago.
Gangster Boogie, BlackBlock/Palais de Tokyo, Paris.
Dzine, Equal Gallery, Osaka, Japan.
Beautiful Things, SCAI the Bathhouse/Shiraishi Contemporary Art Inc., Tokyo.
beautiful otherness, Monique Meloche Gallery, Project Booth, ARCO, Madrid

2003   *alleyoop*, Institute of Visual Arts (INOVA), University of Wisconsin – Milwaukee.
Tokyo Boogie, University of Alabama Museum of Art, Birmingham.
Dzine, Galeria Carlos Irazarry en Candela, San Juan, Puerto Rico.

2002   *beat junkie, chop shop*, Monique Meloche Gallery, Chicago.
Sampler, Museum of Contemporary Art, Chicago, Illinois.

2001   Galerie Porte 2a, Bordeaux, France.
Remix, 111 Minna Gallery, San Francisco, California.
Suckerpunch, Spaces-Spacelab, Cleveland, Ohio.

2000   *The Red Sessions*, Cristinerose Gallery, New York.

1999   *Bossa Trés Jazz 2*, Colette, Paris.
Suckerpunch, CSPS/ Legion Arts, Cedar Rapids, Iowa.
Dzine, Eastwick Gallery, Chicago.

1998   *Dzine*, Maison Francaise-French Cultural Centre, Nairobi, Kenya.

1997   *Dzine*, Heart Galerie, Paris, France.
Dzine, Lydon Fine Art, Chicago.

Selected Group Exhibitions:

2005   *Lost in Music*, JCCC Gallery/Nerman Museum of Contemporary Art,
Overland Park, Kansas

2004   *None of the Above: Contemporary Work by Puerto Rican Aritsts*, Real Art Ways, Hartford,
Connecticut and Museo de Arte de Puerto Rico, Puerto Rico.
Stop & Stor: New Painters, LUXE Gallery, New York.

2003   *Painting by Design*, Wayne State University Gallery, Detroit, Michigan.

2002   StreetwiseOne, A-PART Gallery, London.
Bossa Trés Jazz 2: Step into the Gallery, Galerie Valerie Cueto, Paris.
SK8 on the wall, Rocket Gallery, Tokyo, and traveled to PARCO Gallery, Nagoya, Japan.

2001   *Search For Love: Dj Cam, Dzine, Judy Ledgerwood*, Gallery 312, Chicago. (cd)
Chicago Nascar Project, Museum of Contemporary Art, Chicago, Illinois
Mixer, Monique Meloche Gallery, Chicago.

2000   *Xhibition/Transition*, Chicago.
Homewrecker, Monique Meloche Gallery, Chicago.

1998   *Chicago Artists '98* - Gallery 312, Chicago.

1997   *Eee-motional*, Depaul University Art Gallery, Chicago.
*The Community Collects: Latin American and Latino Art from Private Bay Area
Collections*, the Mexican Museum, San Francisco.
Four Contemporary Artists, The Moore Building, Miami.

1996   *Anna Kunz, John Santoro, Dzine*, Lineage Gallery, Chicago.
Crossing Paths, Galerie Michel Gillet, Paris.

1995   *Healing Walls: Murals and Community, a Chicago History*, Illinois Art Gallery, Chicago
and traveled to Springfield Museum, Springfield, Illinois.

1994   *Aerosoul*, Paterson Museum, Paterson, New Jersey.
Dzine and Mike Lash, Beret international Gallery, Chicago.

1993   *Abstract: Chicago*, Klein Art Works, Chicago.
World Tattoo Gallery, Chicago.
N.A.M.E Gallery, Chicago.

1992   *Poetry in Motion*, Beret International Gallery, Chicago.

Selected Bibliography

Blackshaw, Ric. "StreetwiseOne," *Royal Elastics*, London: Apart Gallery; 2002.
Brathwaite, Fred (a.k.a Fab Five Freddy). "It Ain't Where your From, It's Where you're At" in *Xhibition/
Transtition*, Chicago: Leapnet; 2000.
Cotter, Holland. "Art in Review: None of the Above, Contemporary Art from Puerto Rican Artists" *New York
Times*, June 2004, 29 (B).
Fitzgerald, Shannon. "Dzine: Punk Funk: A Wayward Fusion" in *Dzine: Punk Funk*, St. Louis: Contemporary
Art Museum St. Louis; 2005.
Doroshenko, Peter. "Color Room" in *Dzine*, Osaka, Japan: Equal Gallery; 2004. (limited edition box set
exhibition catalog).
Dzine, *Red Sessions*, catalog w/ music cd (arrangement and artwork by Dzine), Chicago: Ace Graphics and
Yellow Productions, Paris; 2000.
Genocchio, Benjamin. "Puerto Rican Artists, Yes, but with a Global Vision" *New York Times CT* (June 2004): 12.
Ho, Alain. "Dzine: When Music Meets Painting," *Tres…Jazz* , Chicago: Yellow Productions; 1999.
McCormick, Carlo. Forward in *Dzine: New Paintings and Constructions*, Chicago: Eastwick Gallery; 1998.
Meloche, Monique and Jerome Sans. *Sampler*, Chicago: Museum of Contemporary Art; 2002.
Pozuelo, Abel H. "El gran festin de Project Rooms," *El Cultural* (February 2004).
Robinson, Walter. "Report from Madrid," *artnet.com* (February 2004).
Shouse, Heather. "Bucking the System," *CS* (April 2003): 38.
Spiegel, Olga. "Los Project Rooms de Arco…." *La Vangaurdia* (February 2004).
Spiegler, Marc "From Hip Hop Culture to a Global Urban-ism," *Modart Magazine* (May/June 2004).
Spiegler, Marc and Philippe Graff. *Bossa Tres Jazz 2: Step into the Gallery*, Paris: Valerie Cueto Gallery; 2002.
Stein, Lisa. "Artist Profile" *Chicago Tribune Arts & Entertainment* (September 2002): 9 (7).
Warren, Lynne, ed. *Art in Chicago 1945 – 1995*, New York: Thames and Hudson and Museum of Contemporary
Art, Chicago; 1996.

Warren, Lynne. "Dzine for Living", Chicago: published by artist; 1995.
Weinstein, Michael. "Yes, Yes, Y'all: The Birth of Hip Hop" *Dialogue* (March-April 2003): 27.
Yates, Iva. "Art by Contemporary Puerto Rican Artists at MAPR," Cultural Affairs, *Caribbean Business* (January 2005): 43.
Yood, James. "Dzine"in *Lost in Music* exhibition brochure, JCCC Gallery/Nerman Museum of Contemporary Art, Overland Park, Kansas: 2005.
Zambreno, Kate. "The Art of Dzine," *NewCity*, (October 2002): 5-7.

CD projects:

2005	Punk Funk, *The Lost Kingdom*, DJ Cam – sound collaboration, Paris, Chicago and St. Louis.
	Dipper, Real Estate Records, Chicago (cover art).
2004	Gotan Project, Paris - sound collaboration and cover art.
	Classic Recordings, Greens Keepers, Chicago (cover art).
2003	*Om records*, Greens Keepers, Chicago (cover art).
	Libera Mi Alma, Free my Soul, lala Productions Chicago (ltd. edition 12").
	Water Club San Juan, Guidance Recordings/ lala productions, double CD compilation (arrangement and cover art).
2002	*NUSPIRIT HELSINKI*, Guidance Recordings, Chicago (cover art).
2001	*Search for Love*, music CD, sound collaboration with DJ Cam, Guidance Recordings, Chicago.
1999	*Bossa Tres....Jazz*, double c.d & c.d rom - Yellow Productions-East/West, Paris.

Artist residencies and performances:

2002	JUBA Collective, Artists in Residence, Museum of Contemporary Art, Chicago.
	JUBA Collective, Performance: Jazz Lines Festival, Theater im Haus der Kunst, Munich.
2001	JUBA Collective, Artists in Residency, Bordeaux, France.
1991	*Gargolian Books of Stock*, installation and performance with Rammellzee, New York.

Grants and awards:

1999	Andy Warhol Foundation, Artist in Residency-CSPS/Legion Arts, Cedar Rapids, Iowa.
1998	City of Chicago Sister Cities Program (Artist in Residency, Nairobi, Kenya)
1995	National Endowment for the Arts

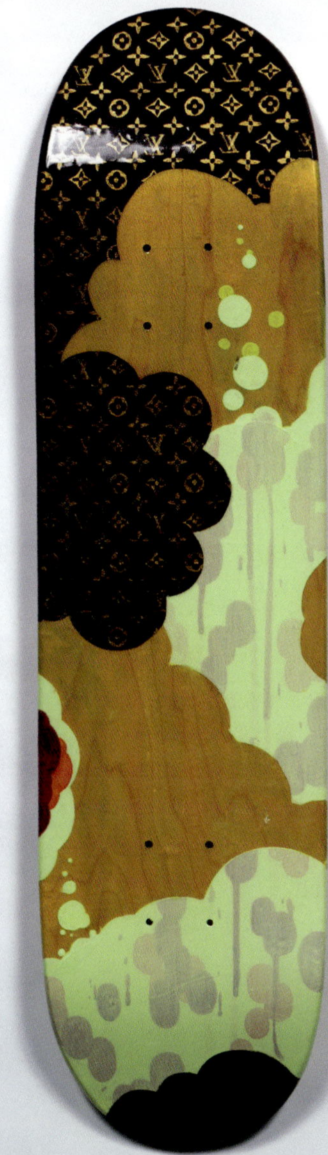
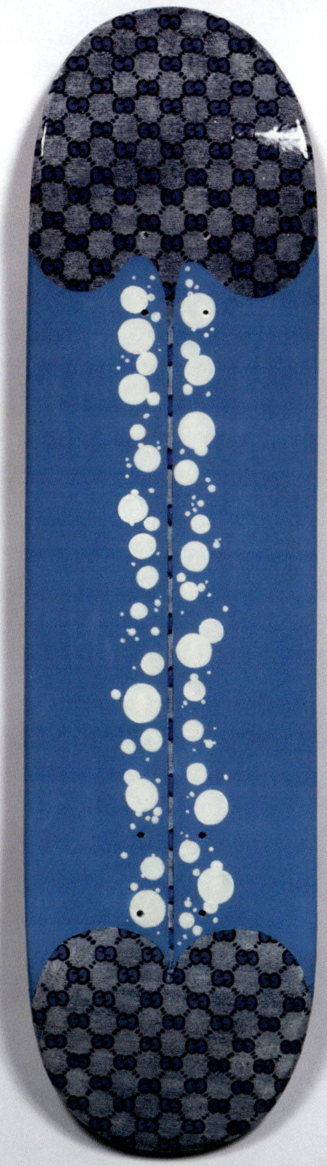

bling 2, 2002 (two skateboards), acrylic and Envirotex on skateboards, diptych; 32 x 8 inches. each. Collection of Glen Saltzberg & Jordana Joseph, Chicago.

DJ Cam Biography

Parisian hip-hop devotee Laurent Daumail (a.k.a. DJ Cam) is part of a short (but growing) list of French artists updating hip-hop for the chill-out crowd, garnering inspiration from the beats and samples of producers like DJ Premier, Prince Paul, and Rakim and layering it with sprinkles of dub, jazz, and soundtrack-y type ambience. His minimalist approach, coupled with downbeat instrumental hip-hop built from obscure samples and stomp-box turntable accompaniments re-birth themselves into artfully arranged compositions bordering on British Acid Jazz. Over the years, DJ Cam has also cultivated a following by remixing projects from everyone from Air to MILES DAVIS and even Michael Jackson.

Cam is now a household name in the underground trip-hop-electronica-ambient community in parts of Europe and Japan in 2002 Cam had his biggest year to date, garnering kudos at the U.K. Hip-Hop Awards where he walked away with the award for Best European Hip-Hop Act. Blurring the lines between R&B, contemporary Jazz, and hip-hop, he released the album 'Soulshine' through Colombia records- "a musical departure which sees a dependence on live musicianship." Featuring the likes of Guru, R&B stalwart Larry Blackmon (Cameo), Dee Brigewater's daughter China, neo-soul singer Donnie, rapper Afu-Ra, and Indonesian female singer Anggun, the album's tracks veered away from any preconceptions of what a pure DJ album should sound like.

As a young child, Cam grew up around music, learning to play several instruments including piano and drums while listening to jazz with his father before discovering the world of turntables. In 1993 he founded the miniscule 'Street Jazz' label and released his debut 'Underground Vibes' in 1994. In 1995 he established Inflammable Records releasing a live project titled the 'Underground Live'. The year 1997 included the release of 'Substances' (on Inflammable Records) followed the next year by 'The Beat Assassinated,' featuring a select array of rappers including Silver Bullet, Channel Live, Otis and Dadou from KDD. The new millennium brought the release of a trilogy titled 'The Loa Projects,' an experimental work aimed at re-capturing the artist's "voodoo spirit." 'Soulshine' furthered this approach, but steered toward a smoother, more organic feel.

In 2004 Cam released his new album "Liquid Hip Hop," back on his Inflamable imprint, is a return to the minimal, old-school hip-hop approach. The album lives up to its title, taking us on a journey through solid breaks, samples and the slinkiest keyboard sounds, all flowing together and blended perfectly by Cam himself. As ever, Cam makes music for the summer; kick back, get a cold drink, and soak it up!

Maya Romanoff Biography

Maya Romanoff is the founder and director of the Chicago-based Maya Romanoff Corporation, one of the most advanced and innovative interior furnishings manufacturers in the world. Romanoff and his firm have transformed modern design by combining ancient artistic techniques and up-to-date industrial production, with a keen appreciation for environmental concerns.

Romanoff is an explorer of new media, developing designs by using his hands on the media itself. The range of media used in what the company calls "wall surfaces," extends to once-unimagined materials for that purpose: rayon, wood, marble, granite, sand, and metal leaf, just to name a few.

His fascination with making things took root during early travels through Africa and Europe and blossomed at that defining event of the 1960s, Woodstock. Following that, Romanoff experimented with techniques that elevated tie-dye garments from hippie attire to haute couture, sold by Henri Bendel in New York and other retail arbiters of high fashion throughout the United States.

The same penchant for making things led Romanoff to a lifetime of experimentation with materials for walls. Along with the artist Christo, Romanoff also helped launch textiles as a medium for contemporary architectural ornamentation on the intimate and the monumental scale. Beginning in the early 1970s, some famous installations include The Harris Music and Dance Theater Chicago at Millennium Park, by Frank Geary (Chicago: 2004), the Chicago *Sun Times* Building (Chicago: 1988), Kyoto City Center (Kyoto City, Japan: 1987), the Pacific Design Center (Los Angeles: 1979), and the Arsenal and Belvedere Castle (both in New York's Central Park: 1978-79).

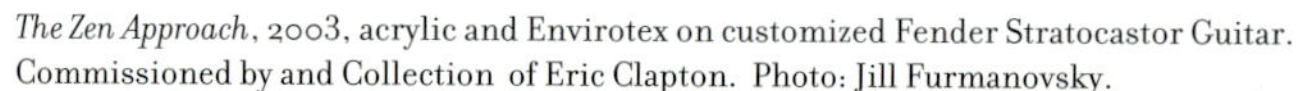

The Zen Approach, 2003, acrylic and Envirotex on customized Fender Stratocastor Guitar.
Commissioned by and Collection of Eric Clapton. Photo: Jill Furmanovsky.

Colophon

This book was designed by Bruce Burton on a MacIntosh G5 in Adobe Indesign. The typefaces are Filosofia and CA Aries. Filosofia, designed by Zuzana Licko in 1996, is an historical revival based on the design of Bodoni and is distributed through Emigre, a digital type foundry, publisher, and distributor of graphic design related software and printed materials based in northern California. CA Aries, designed by Stefan Claudius, was inspired by a postcard from Buenos Aires in the 1930's, and is distributed through www.cape-arcona.com a online type foundry based in Germany.

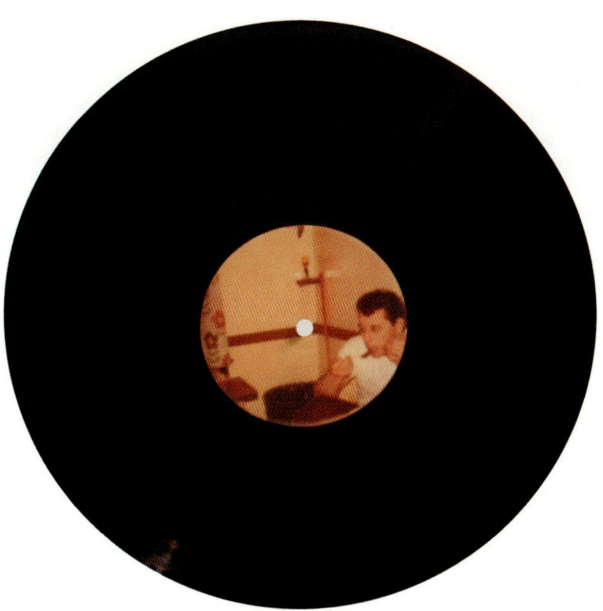

Libera mi Alma, 2003, Limited Edition 12' vinyl record. Produced and directed by Dzine.

following page:
Punk Funk (detail), 2005. Contemporary Art Museum St. Louis. Photo: Bruce Burton.

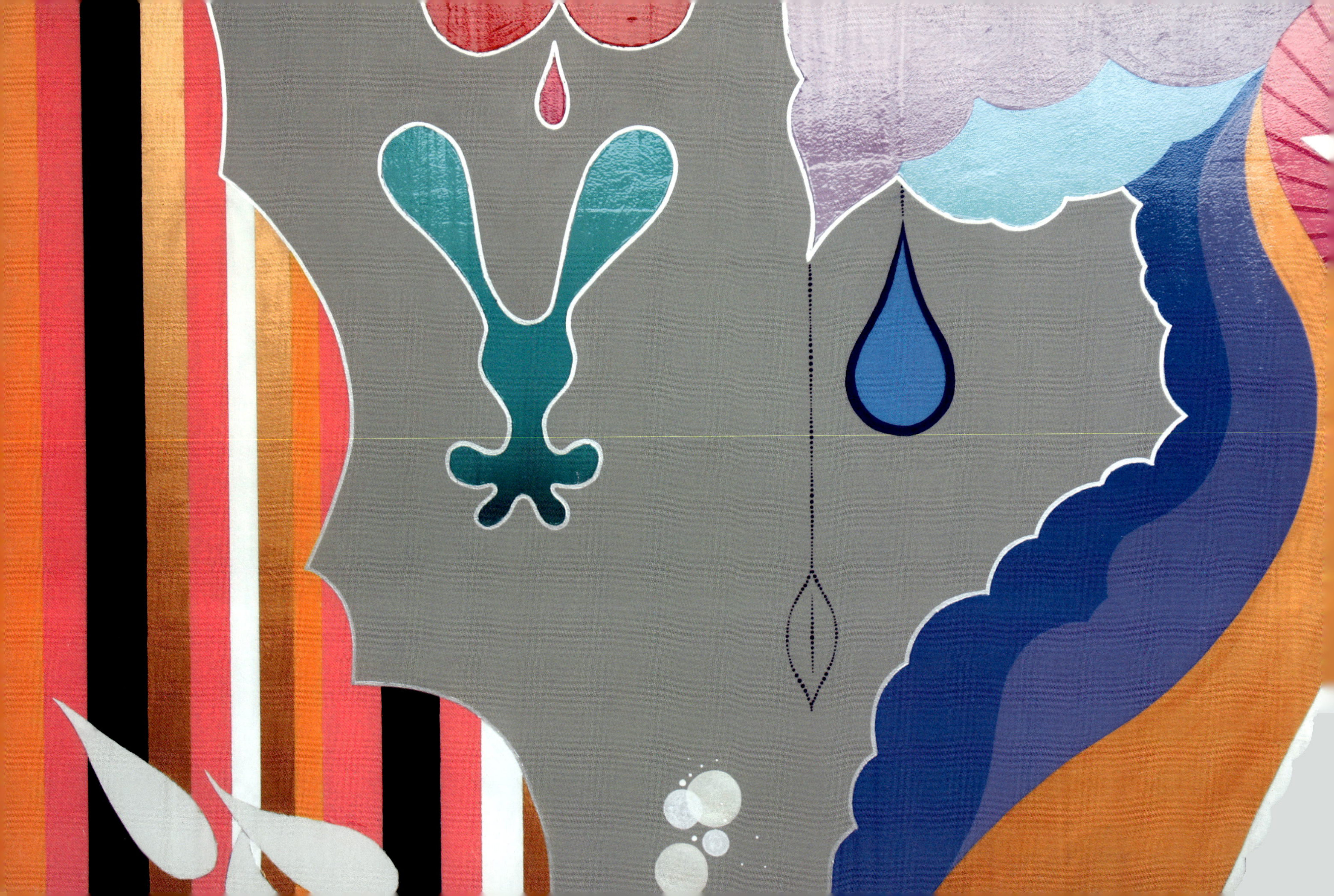